THE FURTHER READING LIBRARY

LOÏE FULLER
LECTURE ON RADIUM

THOMAS WILFRED
CLAVILUX AND LUMIA HOME MODELS

RICHARD SHARPE SHAVER
SOME STONES ARE ANCIENT BOOKS

RICHARD FOREMAN
NO TITLE

MARGARET WATTS HUGHES
SOUND MAY BE SEEN

JACKIE GLEASON
LIBRARY OF THE PARANORMAL

TONY SCHWARTZ
SNAPSHOTS IN SOUND

CHARLES FORT
RESEARCH

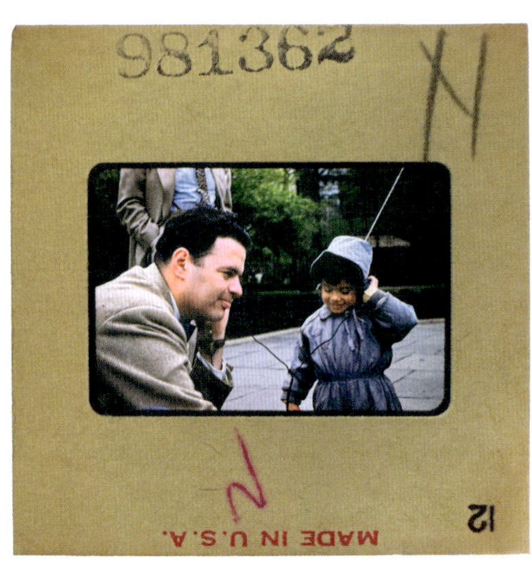
981362
MADE IN U.S.A.
12

TONY SCHWARTZ

SNAPSHOTS IN SOUND

CHRISTINE BURGIN BOOKS

THE FURTHER READING LIBRARY

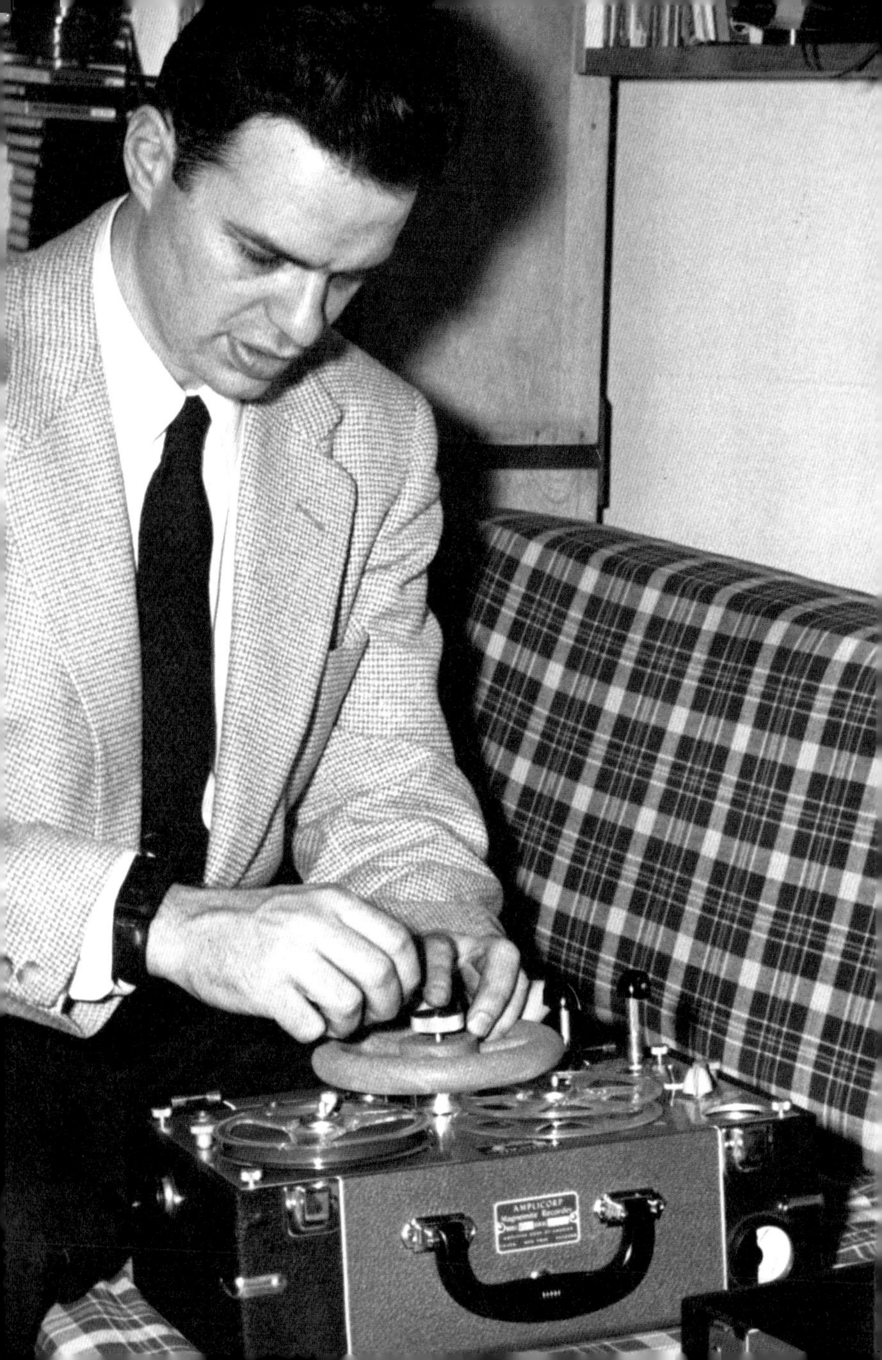
AMPLICORP
Magnetic Recorder

COMMUNICATING WITH TAPE

Tony Schwartz

HIFI/STEREO REVIEW, MARCH 1962

Most people today use the tape recorder in a way that seems to me to be self-limiting, if not actually self-defeating. They will buy a portable recorder that is capable of recording the sounds of life anywhere and then use it only as a copying device to record sounds from the radio, sounds from records, sounds from television. With due recognition of the values, including the pleasures, of taping performances of great music from broadcasts and other sources, the tape recorder has a much greater potential; using a tape recorder only for copying musical performances is rather like using a camera only to photograph paintings in an art museum or photographs in a magazine. But most people seldom use it in the way that it seems to me would be most rewarding and most enriching: to record sounds expressive of their own unique interests and involvements.

The common view of the tape recorder as a mere copying instrument is not so surprising when you consider that this is the view promoted by the manufacturers of such equipment. To illustrate this, two stories come to mind. A number of years

Tony Schwartz with portable tape recorder, ca. 1956

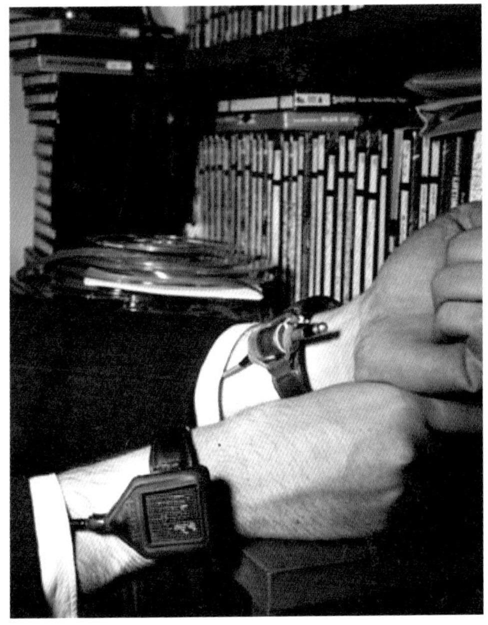

The small Brush microphone is attached to the right wrist with a strap. The wire from the mike runs up to the sleeve, across his back and down the left sleeve, terminating in a plug which fits the mike input on the recorder. Part of his huge tape collection can be seen in the background where racks extend from floor to ceiling.

ago I purchased one of the early models of a now famous recorder. It was lighter than most recorders available at that time, and I wanted to use it to record sounds and situations on location. I took my new machine out into the New York subway, and, to my surprise, I found that the loud squeal of the trains' brakes could not be recorded properly while following the built-in recording meter. I wrote the manufacturer's engineering department, and they wrote back that their machine had a twenty-decibel boost in its recording equalization on the high end and that if I wanted to record a high-volume, high-frequency sound on their machine I should not record at full volume, but at twenty decibels below zero level—a level not visible on their recording meter. They also said that to do this it would be wise to anticipate the problem by carefully following the score. I wrote back that since the subway did not publish a score I would have to solve the problem some other way. I bought a different recorder.

Another manufacturer of a self-powered portable machine put the recording-level meter inside the case, which, of course, had to be opened to read the dial. Evidently he did not conceive of using his recorder while moving about. I took his recorder, moved the meter to the outside top of the case, cut holes in the case over the controls, installed an outside microphone jack, added a leather shoulder strap and finally had the first really portable recorder in the country.

Lately I have seen advertisements that begin to speak of tape recording in the way I think of it. "Take snapshots in sound!"

Description of Schwartz's wrist worn microphone used for field recording, from liner notes of Sounds of My City, *Folkways Records, 1956*

"Be able to capture your trip!" "Put sounds with your slides!" Phrases like these, I think, inspire people to use their recorders in a more rewarding manner.

Life is an inexhaustible reservoir of material to be recorded and listened to. The whole world of non-musical sound and the spoken word has been approached very narrowly until now. Putting plays, readings by poets, and the voices of famous people on tape and records is a wonderful thing indeed, but enterprises of this sort amount to very little compared to what there is to be recorded.

Most magazines that deal with the recording field deal with it only on a technical level, with no discussion of the philosophy or theory, no human reaction to the act of recording in a free, full emotional sense. In this they are very different from the photography magazines. For example, the kind of comment that follows, from *Popular Photography*, is as familiar in photography journalism as it is foreign to publications dealing with sound:

"Every photograph is really giving a personal visual report on something. Whether it's Smirnoff's Vodka or the new model Mercedes-Benz or some event on the street or something in the headlines, the problem of the photographer is to discover his own language, a visual ABC's to explain this event. The photograph is not only a pictorial report; it is also a psychological report. It represents the feelings and point of view of the intelligence behind the camera."

Yet actually the tape recorder has a history and potential very similar to those of the camera, especially the thirty-five-millimeter camera, and those who are interested in communicating with sound through tape and tape recording can learn a tremendous amount from photography. As the great photographer Edward Steichen said in 1936, "The lens records with equal fidelity the trite, the superficial, and the significant. It is the photographer's perception that must differentiate." Much the same could be said of the tape recorder and the art of the creative recordist.

Today we have an increasing awareness of photography as an art form. Many prominent museums are including photographs in their collections. We recognize literature, painting, sculpture, music, dance, theater, and photography as art forms, but so far no recognition has been given to the art form of recording. You will hear the term "the art of recording," but when you scratch below the surface you find that what is really meant is the science or technique of recording, and that the only thing really considered an art is the music being recorded.

Magnetic recording makes it possible for a middle-income person to undertake projects that were previously limited to well-endowed institutions. In the course of living we come across many subjects that are worthy of study and presentation in audible form. Many such studies fall within the interest of organized foundations, record companies, or the broadcast industry. Others, for various reasons, do not interest or cannot be handled by them, and it is left for individuals to investigate these untouched areas of study, which he can do without accepting various forms of restriction and censorship that may be imposed by institutions or industry. When I speak of censorship, I do not mean government censorship. I simply mean the censorship implied in judgments such as "Does this have commercial value?" and "Will anyone object to this?" The only restrictions the individual must deal with are those implicit in the limitations of our minds, talents, and equipment.

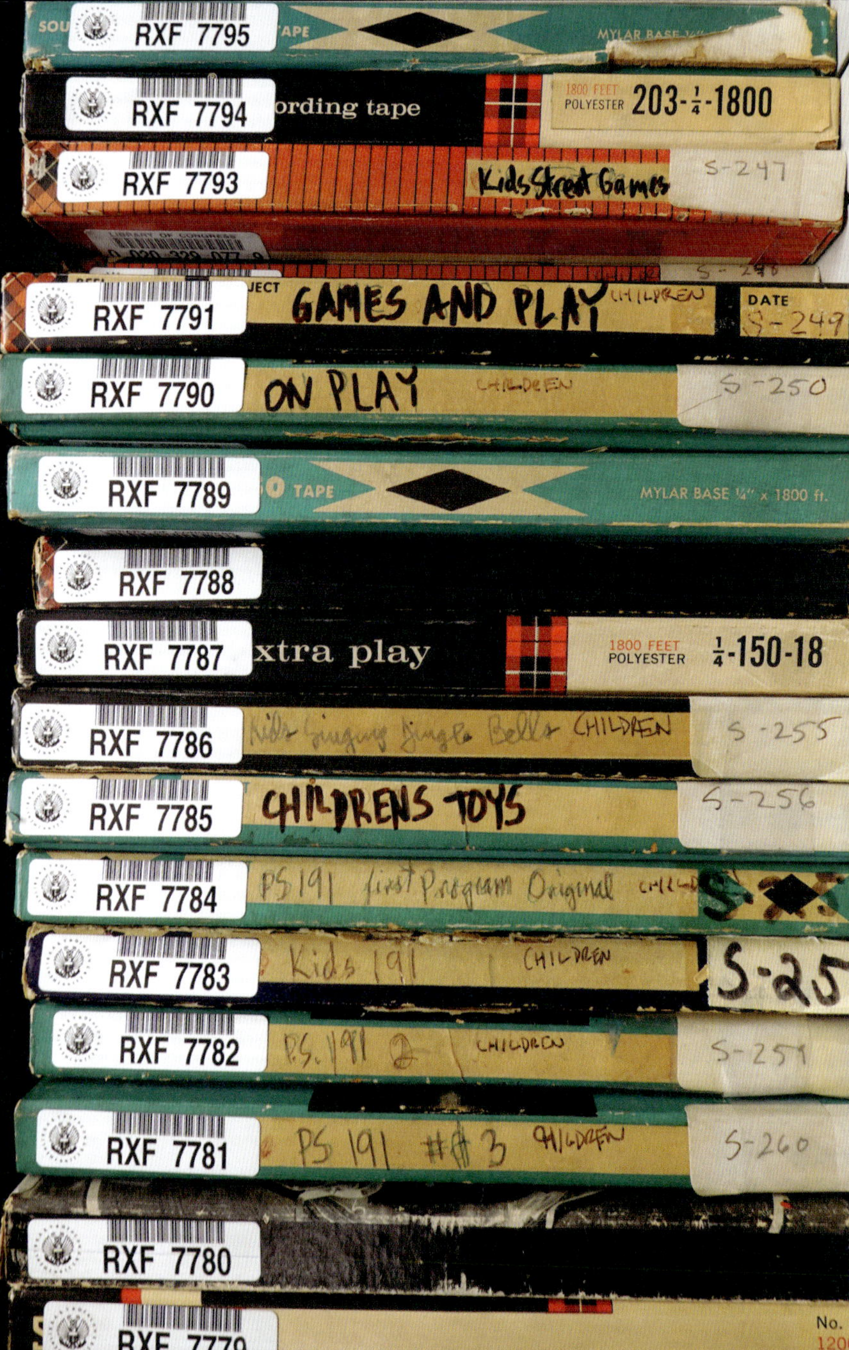

RXF 7795
TAPE
MYLAR BASE
RXF 7794
ording tape
1800 FEET
POLYESTER
203-$\frac{1}{4}$-1800
RXF 7793
Kids Street Games
S-247
RXF 7791
GAMES AND PLAY
CHILDREN
DATE
S-249
RXF 7790
ON PLAY
CHILDREN
S-250
RXF 7789
TAPE
MYLAR BASE ¼" x 1800 ft.
RXF 7788
RXF 7787
xtra play
1800 FEET
POLYESTER
$\frac{1}{4}$-150-18
RXF 7786
Kids Singing Jingle Bells CHILDREN
S-255
RXF 7785
CHILDRENS TOYS
S-256
RXF 7784
PS 191 first Program Original
RXF 7783
Kids 191
CHILDREN
S-25
RXF 7782
P.S. 191 2
CHILDREN
S-25
RXF 7781
PS 191 #3
CHILDREN
S-260
RXF 7780
RXF 7779
No. 2
1200

A person can have aural reactions to sounds and situations, both real and abstract, that he can record, organize, blend, superimpose, and finally present to other people and re-create in them some of the feeling he has had about the original sounds and situations. The time will come when sound, not necessarily music, will be recorded, formed, and preserved on tape, disc, or plastic page and when these will be kept in homes, libraries, schools, and museums for repeated listening.

I am interested in preserving the audible expression of material as an expression of people and their way of life. I do my recording while going about my everyday life, always carrying a small portable recorder with me so that I can make a high-fidelity recording of any situation I am in, or near, within fifteen seconds from the start of my awareness of it. My job may take me to a printer's shop. The sounds, situations, and language of a trade can be recorded in just a few extra minutes of the required job time. The ride to work can produce a recording of a cab or bus driver talking about his work or other aspects of his life. The walk home from dinner at a restaurant can yield a recording of a street preacher or musician. A Saturday morning walk to the supermarket can yield three or four children's games or jump rope rhymes.

I have found the best approach with children as well as with adults is to be honest with them. Identification with and understanding of people is the key to many rich recordings. For instance, if I want to do a study of an aspect of children's

Audiotapes in the Tony Schwartz Collection at the Library of Congress, Packard Campus for Audio Visual Conservation, Culpeper, Virginia

lives—say their invisible playmates—I try to get honestly involved with the children and to record them speaking about these friends and playing with them and also to record the reactions of people who know the children. Out of all this, I pattern the story I want to tell.

In general, then, I consider my recordings as means of expression and communication, with programs that express ideas and feelings about the life around me. I feel that they are complete when people understand my emotion and respond with some of the feeling that I myself have about the subject of the recording. I do not believe that such programs can be rushed in production; recording projects, like children, need understanding, work, time, and love to grow to maturity.

A list of some of the sound stories and records I have worked [on] over the last few years will give you an idea of the possibilities of sound communication:

"Sounds of My City," a story of New York as heard through the sounds of its people and things; "Children's Street Songs and Games"; "New York 19," a study of the folklore of a midtown Manhattan Postal Zone; "Millions of Musicians," a study of the innate musicality of people; "Music on the Streets"; "The World in My Mailbox," a world-wide tape exchange; "The New York Taxi Driver"; "The History of a Voice," a study of the development of a voice over eleven years and its relationship to three generations; "Christmas in New York"; and so on.

Audiotapes in the Tony Schwartz Collection including recordings of Moondog and of Schwartz's niece Nancy that he used to create the audio piece "Nancy Grows Up" (aka "The History of a Voice")

653

731 Downbeat Music 10-11-52

NANCY Schwartz 5-10-52

Nancy Nov 8, 52

Nancy
8-22-53

Nadler on TAXIS in Paris

MOONDOG ON STREET
#2 (GOOD)

In projects like these you can use either plug-in recorders or the newer battery-operated portables. To show you how a project develops, I will tell the story of "The History of a Voice."

A little over ten years ago, my brother phoned me at work and said, "Sheila is going to the hospital. Can you make it?" Sixty minutes later, from the corridor outside the nursery I was recording the sounds made by my very first niece. She was twenty minutes old.

For the first six months, I recorded Nancy every week or two—her cries, her coos, her burps, her chortles. As she grew, her ability to communicate through sound grew. At nine months, she was using the sounds of words she heard, and at fourteen months, she began to talk somewhat coherently.

As the years went by, Nancy's world changed and was accordingly reflected in her talk. At three years, she talked about toys, at four she talked about dogs, at six about satellites, and at nine about Girl Scout Camp. After two years with Nancy, I was aware of the possibilities of her "sound portrait" and started to think of other ways of broadening the material I had on tape. As I listened to what I had recorded, it reminded me of collections of pictures that showed whole family groups—brothers, sisters, parents, and grandparents. So I decided to record the voices of Nancy's parents and grandparents. From all the material I accumulated (which I kept on a few large reels of tape labelled "Nancy"), I took representative selections of Nancy's sounds and comments that showed her at various intervals as she grew. To these I added sounds and voices from her family and so assembled a sound portrait of Nancy. I am still recording Nancy every few months, and every year new leaves appear on the family tree.

Another sound story with an interesting background is "The Sound of Sculpture." One day a friend called and said that he was going to the Museum of Modern Art to photograph a Swiss artist, Jean Tinguely. Mr. Tinguely was building a three-dimensional work called *Homage to New York*. Constructed from old bicycle and carriage wheels, pianos, tin cans, steel rods, rolls of paper, electric motors, bottles, saws, and so on, it was conceived to be constructed, set in motion, run a while, and, within thirty minutes, start to destroy itself and finally collapse completely.

I went to the museum with my friend, met Mr. Tinguely, and watched him work on his sculpture in the geodesic dome in the garden behind the museum. As he worked and talked to us, I thought it would be interesting to do a sound story on his unusual work. I recorded him there, telling us of his intent and methods. I also recorded the sounds of his work and the sounds of the moving parts of the sculpture, returning a few times during the weeks of work that followed and continued to record. Finally, exhibition day came. Several hundred people were invited to see his work come to life, live, and die. The press and television crews were there to cover the event, too. I recorded Mr. Tinguely in his hour of glory. I recorded the museum director, the individual and group reactions of the spectators, the firemen who were there to protect the museum, and, of course, the sounds of the sculpture itself. From all the material, I blocked out an order of presentation, wrote a narration that bound the segments, and then recorded and mixed my sound story "The Sound of Sculpture."

Many of the situations you and I come upon in our daily living can be recorded and made into sound stories, but there

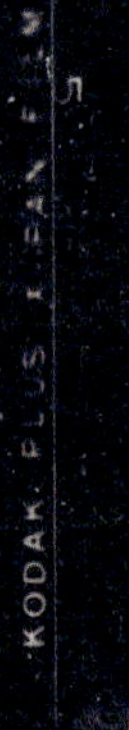
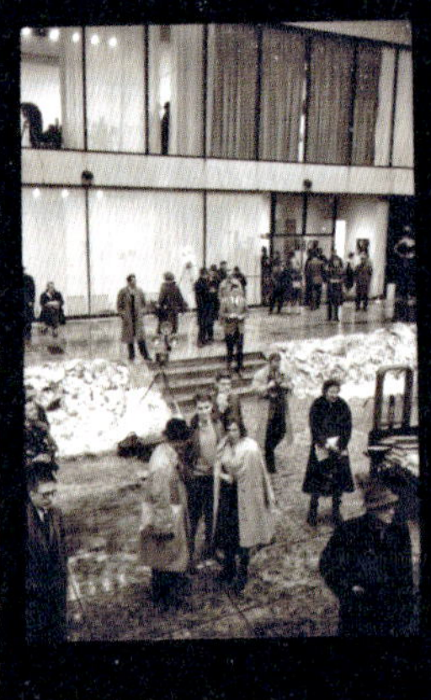
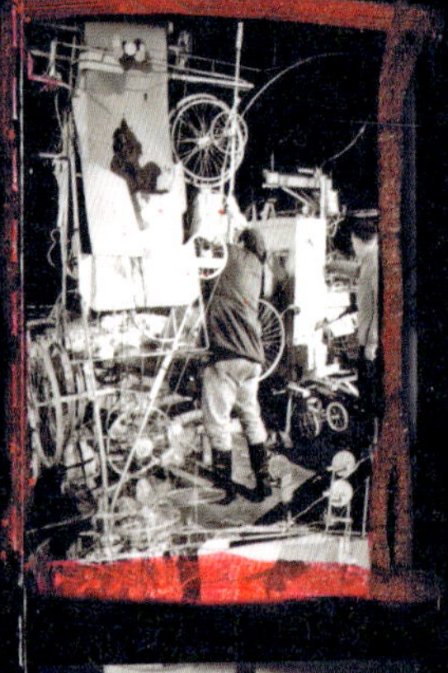
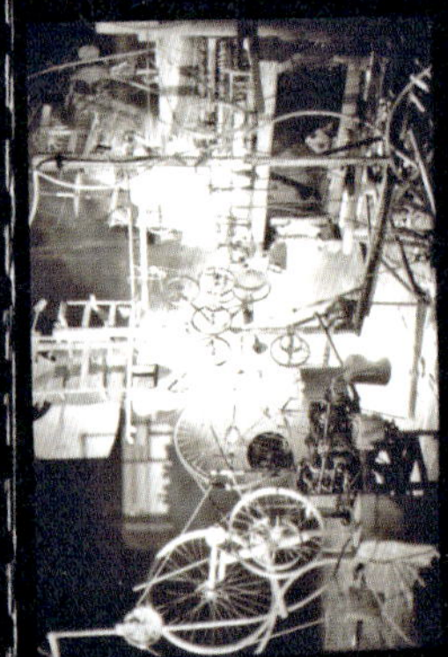

are no places that can teach one how to record. Nevertheless, magazines like this can make certain helpful suggestions—for instance, that anyone who wants to work creatively with tape should only record in one direction. This is necessary whether your recorder is a full-, half-, or quarter-track machine if you are to have the freedom to cut and remove sections of tape and arrange them in the order you desire. If you record in both directions, as you edit one track you would automatically cut and destroy the other.

Of course you want to have the best technique you can have, but if you learn only technique you will become only a technician. Still, you must master the technique first of all. I think of a comment by the great photographer Edward Weston: "One does not think during creative work any more than one thinks when driving a car. But one has a background of years—learning, unlearning, success, failure, dreaming, thinking, experience, all this—then the moment of creation, the focusing of all into the moment."

Selections from the photographer Ken Heyman's contact sheets of the self-destruction of Jean Tinguely's Homage to New York, *Museum of Modern Art Sculpture Garden, New York, March 1960. Visible at left: Tinguely with his work predestruction, Robert Rauschenberg, John Cage, Alfred Leslie, and the final conflagration.*

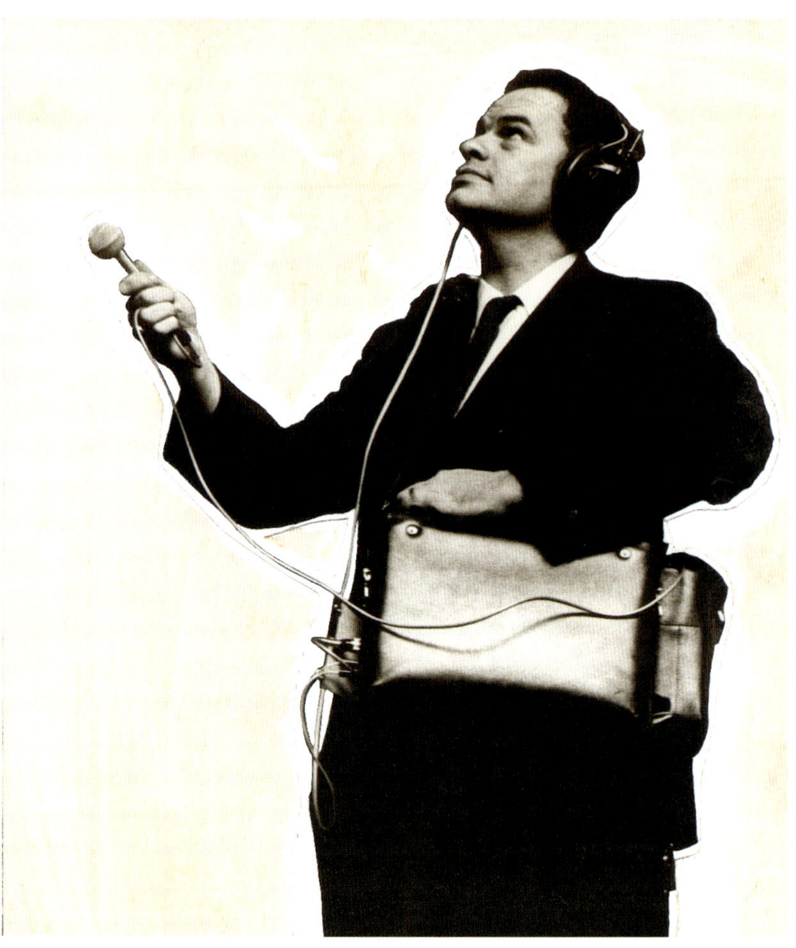

The Tony Schwartz Collection at the Library of Congress contains more than 6,000 audiotapes and videotapes. Their diverse content includes decades of field recordings, mostly made in Schwartz's neighborhood on Manhattan's west side; edited masters and working materials for his radio shows; and recordings created for advertising and political clients ranging from Lyndon Baines Johnson and Jimmy Carter to Maxwell House and Dream Whip. The Schwartz Collection also includes photographs, inventories, manuscripts, and numerous items documenting his wide-ranging activities.

What follows is an A-to-Z overview of Schwartz's encyclopedic work as drawn from this vast archive. Each letter of the alphabet is represented by a sampling of recordings listed in the Library of Congress catalogue. The titles and descriptors of the recordings are copied from Schwartz's handwritten notes on the original tape boxes and reels. These lists are accompanied by resonant selections from within the collection, alphabetically arranged. There are typed descriptions of Schwartz's show "Adventures in Sound" (also known as "Around New York") that ran on WNYC from 1945 to 1976; selected covers of the records he released in the 1950s and '60s (a discography can be found on pages 83–85); images of the original tapes in the Library of Congress vaults; vintage photos showing Schwartz in the field; and floor plans of his tape-filled brownstone home, to name a few.

Undated image from the Tony Schwartz Collection

RP-112-R WNYC AFTER DINNER JOKES

5:48 11/15/66

The tape recorder gives the ability to observe the functioning of people. Observe the use of jokes at a luncheon! Marshal Mcluhan analyses his own jokes; on Churchil speaking french, on a mouse being chased by a bilingual cat, and on a "Help Beautify Junkyards" sign. Good jokes are grievances.

RP-428-R NPR AUDITORY ILLUSION

2:50 5/6/75

Communication Journal. The word "grey" is repeated over and over. A young man comments on what he hears. A ventriloquist says that he thinks "b" but says "d." We are not quite sure what Bob Dylan says when his music is played backwards.

A

A Doctor Who Deals with Affection and Infection
A New Type of Traffic Report
Absolute Sounds
Accidents 1971
After Dinner Jokes
Agoraphobia, Subliminal Tape Program
Air Conditioning
Airport Sounds, Air Raid Sounds
American Talkers
AMIR-Answering Machine Tests
Andrea—Phonomontage
Angel Telling Tony How to Work the Alarm System
Anger
Anton, Camp Calls
Anton Class Play 1976-9-6
Applause at Different Events and Environments
Arlo Guthrie
Assorted Telephone Conversations
Attempt to Call Doctor Line, Roosevelt/St. Luke's Hospital, 1988-12-04
Attitudes and the Subway
Auditory Illusion
Automobile Horns

RP-149-R WNYC BLIND WOMAN STREET SINGER

3:37 4/20/71

A blind female street singer sings as she walks down the street. Maybeen Martin is her name, Missouri was her home. She laughs at the thought of a street singer owning a cadillac; she used to be on welfare. She sings a song from Missouri; "Honey when I die, don't you wear no black!"

B

Baby Cries
Baby on Floor
Bach on Harmonicas
Backyard Clothesline
Bag All Garbage
Bald-Headed Baby
Beefalo
Bell Labs Voice Experimentation
Bella Abzug Tapes
Ben Shahn, Tony Schwartz, and Others Discuss Sound and Lettering 1964-07-14
Big Ben Tolling 12 Times
Big Bill Broonzy
Bill Moyers's Commentary on Tony Schwartz's Daisy Ad
Black-lunged, Stained-tooth, Stinky-haired, Tobacco Toker, Erin McDonald, 12th Grade
Blind News Dealer
Blind Woman Street Singer
Bluegrass and Moe
Bob Gibson Leads a Group of Singing Kids
Bob Landers, Radio Shack, 1979-02
Body Sounds
Boxing (reel #6)
Bruce Logan, Bribery, and City Food Inspectors
Buckminster Fuller Speech and Discussion 1979-02-24
Building Sounds
Bums
Bus Sounds
Buying Old Suit

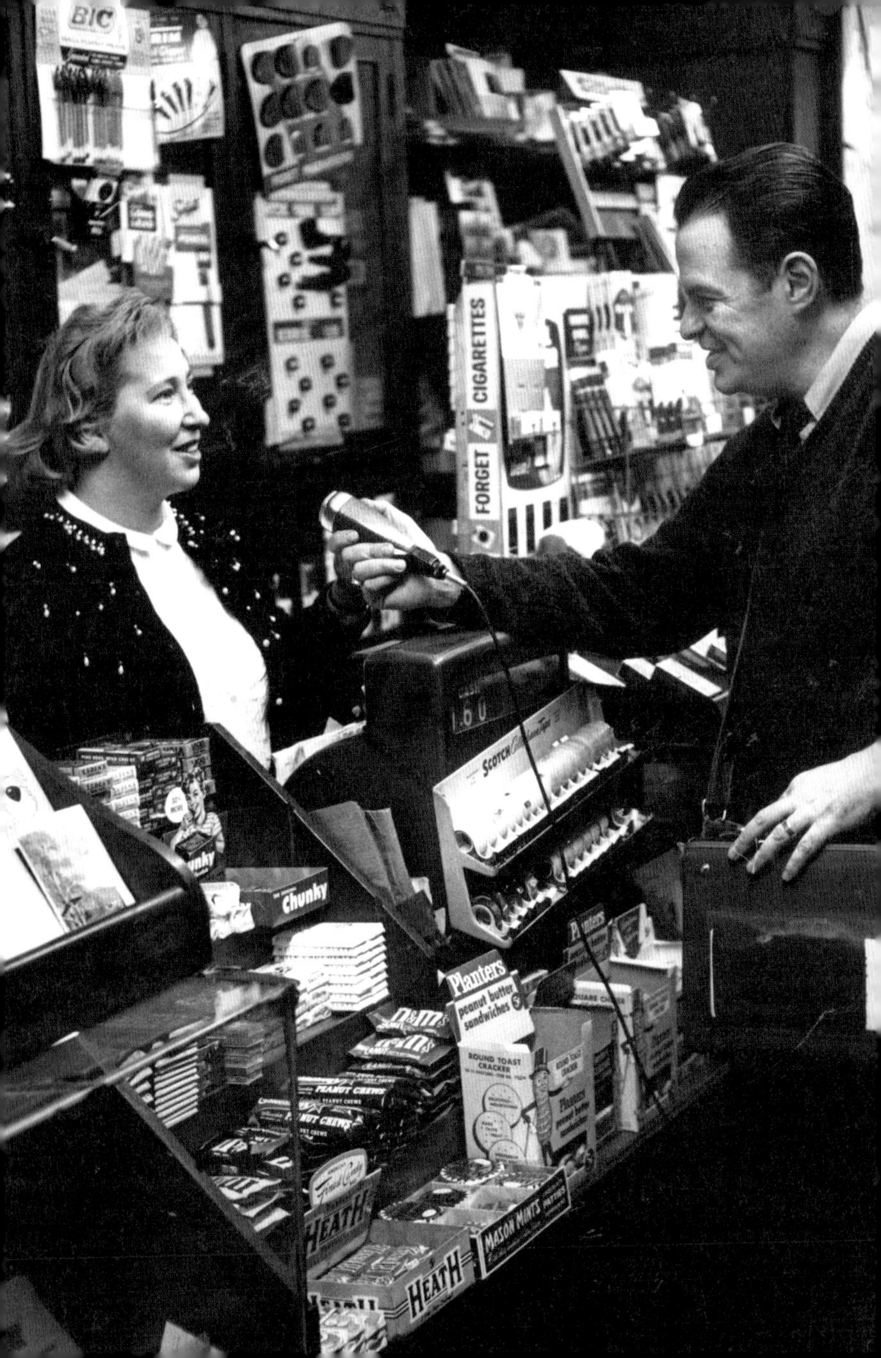
BIC
FORGET
CIGARETTES
SCOTCH
Chunky
Chunky
Planters
peanut butter sandwiches
ROUND TOAST CRACKER
PEANUT CHEWS
HEATH
HEATH
MASON MINTS

C

Candy Store Song
Card Game
Carousels
Casa Galicia
Cataloging Tony's Stuff, 1984-05-14
Chain Gang
Chain-Saw Special Effects
Changes in a Voice
Chapstick
Chewing Gum Songs
Chimney Sweep Ads
Chinese Kuomintang Song
Chinese Restaurant
Coffee—Buying, Grinding, and Making It
Cold Remedies
Columbus Day Parade
Comments on Objects at the Museum of Modern Art
Communist Oath
Confused Speech
Construction Sounds #2
Contact Microphone
Conversation about Mr. Butt's Strip
Country Auction (Vegetables)
Country Night
Crime and Fear in New York, 1959–1965
Crying 1972-02-25

COMMERCIAL ADVERTISING TAPES: C-D

Calgonite	(Dishwasher detergent)	1
Canada Dry	(Soft drinks)	2
Canadian Centennial	(Public Service Promotion)	4
Canadian Nat'l Railroad	(Travel promotional)	4
Carlsberg	(Beer)	2
Carr Stores	(Department Stores)	1
Certs	(Breath Mints)	4
Chapstick	(Lip Balm)	1
Chef Boyardee	(Italian foods)	4
Chemical New York	(Bank)	1
Chrysler	(Automobiles)	3
Chux	(Diapers)	1
City Univ. of New York	(Public Service)	8
Clairol	(Cosmetics)	39
Clinoril	(Arthritis pain reliever)	1
Coldine	(Children's cold reliever)	2
Coldtab	(Children's cold medicine)	1
Columbia Records	(Records)	2
Connecticut Bank & Trust	(Bank)	2
Connecticut General	(Insurance)	1
Consumer Reports	(Magazine)	1
Contac	(Hayfever capsules)	2
Crayola	(Crayons)	1
Creative Growth	(Fund Solicitation)	1
Creative Playthings	(Toys)	2
Creative Surgical Group	(Cosmetic Surgery)	1
Crest	(Toothpaste)	1
C.W.Post Center of L.I.U.	(Student recruiting)	8
Cystic Fibrosis	(Fund solicitation)	1
Misc. "C" :	(Includes Chantilly, Cavanaughs, Colt 45, Colonial Provisions, Citgo)	2
Daily News	(Newspaper)	102
Dancin'	(Play)	1
Data General	(Employee Recruiting)	4
Democratic Nat'l Committee	(Fund solicitation)	3
Dessinex	(Foot powder)	1
Diaperene	(Baby powder)	1
District 1199 Hospital Wrkrs	(Employee Union)	3
Dixie Cup	(Paper cups)	1
Dixie Peach	(Hair dressing)	1
Dream Whip	(Dessert topping)	2
Draino	(Drain cleaner)	1
Drydock Savings Bank	(Bank)	4
Durene	(Fabric)	1
Dutch Bulb	(Plant bulbs)	1
Dutchess Co. Residents	(Citizens' Committee)	2
Misc. "D" :	(Includes Diamond Studs, Dove, Dateline, Duz, Dromedary Date, Duncan Hines)	2

RP-341-R WNYC A COUNTRY NIGHT

3:48 9/24/68

A program dedicated to young people who have never stayed up all night in the country. After the sun goes down, peepers and crickets talk to each other, a dog barks at a passing car, an airplane flies overhead, a bullfrog croaks for a friend, a distant train whistles, the thunder makes the loudest sound, the birds wake up and whistle as day breaks, and a rooster crows good morning.

AN ACTUAL STORY IN SOUND OF

a dog's life

AS BROADCAST ON THE CBS RADIO WORKSHOP

CONCEIVED AND RECORDED BY

TONY SCHWARTZ

PHOTOS BY KEN HEYMAN

NARRATED BY RALPH BELL NARRATION WRITTEN BY ELLIOTT GRUSKIN PRODUCED BY PAUL ROBERTS

FD 5580 **FOLKWAYS RECORDS AND SERVICE CORP., N.Y.** FD 5580

D

Dalton Trumbo Testimony and Interview
Day Workers Bedtime
Death of a Turtle
Dentists, 1960–1961
Depression
Dial Services
Diana's First Budget
Different Reactions to a Bufferin Commercial
Directions to Apple Farm
Dog's Life, CBS Radio Workshop Presentation, 1956
Don't Smoke Rap Song, Andre Speed, Alberta B. G. Schultz Middle School, Hempstead, N.Y.
Door to the Mind
Doorman
Doors and Doorbells
Dosage Recommendations
Dr. Jagendorf and Cabbie Talk About Women
Dr. Manuel Zane on Phobias
Drilling
Drug Names, 1969
Drug Store
Duet with Footsteps, Jimmy Giuffre

RP-53-R WNYC THE ELECTRONIC PITCHMAN

3:44 2/16/71

We used to have an auditory environment which we could see in the street; fish salesmen chanting, the charcoal salesperson, the Makerel seller,.........etc.

Now sound travels at 186,000 miles per second into the homes of people all over the world. Though, sounds can still evoke other sences. Examples from various comercials are included.

E

Edison Cylinders
Edith Lee Discussion with Tony Schwartz about Hard Times in New York City, 1973
Eight O'Clock Coffee, Dinner Party
Eighty-Eighth Street Trees
Electric Circus
Electronic Pitchman
Elevator Operators
Elizabeth Connie Converse
Endorsements of Tony Schwartz's Skill in Designing Commercials
Equinox Gym, Unidentified Voice
Esophageal Speech and Natives of Dutch New Guinea
Esther L. Schwartz and Tony Schwartz Telephone Conversations, 1952, 1961
Evil Conf. Announcement/Garage Door Squeals, 1987-10
Examples of Strange Pronunciations; Conversation with Anton Schwartz
Expressions from Trade or Work (e.g., jazz musicians)

RP-3-R WNYC FOLK SOUNDS

3:55 7/29/69

Folk festivals are doing well but folk sounds can not always be performed. Some folk sounds from many years ago; 1914 car horn, the 3rd Avenue "L" , water dripping into ice pan, screen door,spring creeking, and a coal shoot.

RP-443-R WBAI FRIEDA BERLANT

15:00 10/7/62

Sounds of New York. The sound of fog horns is heard. Frieda Berlant tells about Scotland and about women working in the factories. Her mother told her that the iron in her soup came from the "T" bridge. Frieda remembers a childhood game. She sings a song and explains its meaning. She recites a beautiful poem. Frieda tells how her Jewish folks got to Scotland from Russia. Tony tells about an elderly American Indian woman who has just seen the ocean for the first time. She was invited East by a friend of Tony's. Frieda says a line that her mother used to say; "Your hair's a wee bit fatulte."

F

Fat & Skinny, 1978-10
Father Culkin on Tony Schwartz & Marshall McLuhan
Favorite Sounds
Fifteen Years Ago Today
Fire Engines
Fire Hydrants
Fire in Apartment
Fireplace Sounds
Flight Comments
Fog on the Hudson
Folk Sounds
Footsteps #1
Footsteps #2
Footsteps #3
Fortune Telling, 1962-11
Fragment of a Speech About Personal Computers
Franco-American Spaghetti, Father and Daughter Eat Spaghetti
Frank Mouris
French Adults Talking About Children's Games
Frieda Berlant

G

Gambling Sounds and Discussion About the Lottery
Games and Play
Garbage Truck Sounds
Garment Industry Sounds
Gay Rights Rally, Sheridan Square, NYC, 1979-05-04
Generation Gap
George Leung Singing Chinese Folk Songs
German Beer Hall Nickelodeon
German Clockmaker
Gladys Lea Discussion About President Lyndon B. Johnson and About Cats, 1964
Glass Bowls
Good Chopin
Grafitti [*sic*], 1972-08-25
Great New Fad
Guitar Maker
Guns & Cigarettes, Underground Movement, WMCA, 1988-10-19

H

Hair Today
Hambone Kids
Handwriting Analysis
Happiness No. 4
Happy Birthday from Tony, 1949-12-18
Harry Belafonte 1952-06-18
Harvard Class, 1987-03-17
Having a Baby
Head and Neck Injuries
Hearing in Context, 1971-03-12
Hear-Sight
Heartbeats
Hilton Hotel, 1963-06-15
H. L. Mencken Discussion of His Life as a Reporter and Writer
Holdup witness, 1976-06
Homage to New York
Home Remedies
Horse Sounds, 1960-04
House, 453 W. 56th St., 1962
House Painters 1967-06-06
House Sounds (inside & out)
House Un-American Activities
How Do You Feel About New York?
How to Get Along with Animals, Zookeeper
Humphrey Bogart at The Friars Club
Hypnotist, 1971-02-06

PAGES 37–39: *Floor plans for Tony Schwartz's tape-filled home and studio on West 56th Street, New York*

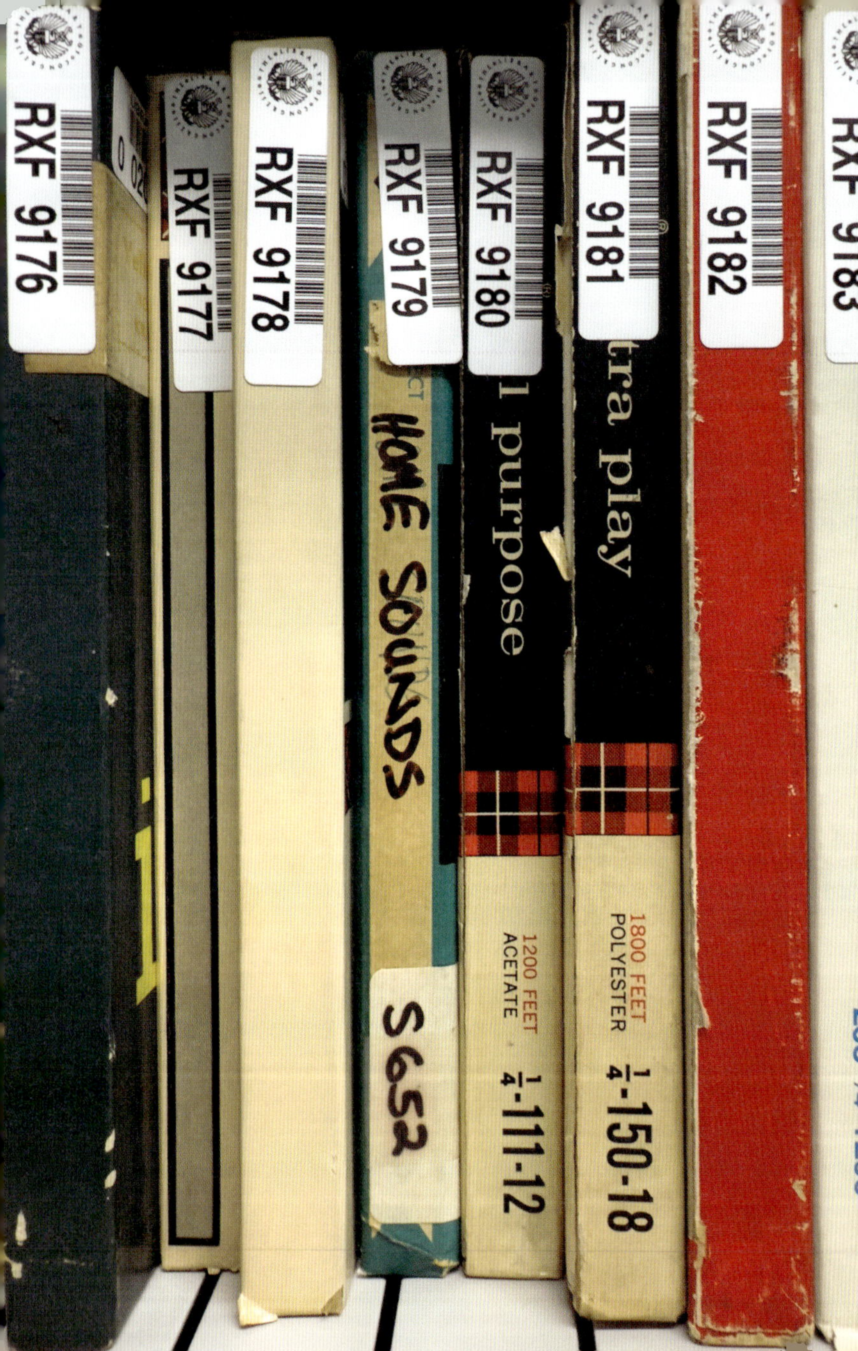
RXF 9176
RXF 9177
RXF 9178
RXF 9179
HOME SOUNDS
S652
RXF 9180
purpose
1200 FEET
ACETATE
1/4-111-12
RXF 9181
tra play
1800 FEET
POLYESTER
1/4-150-18
RXF 9182
RXF 9183

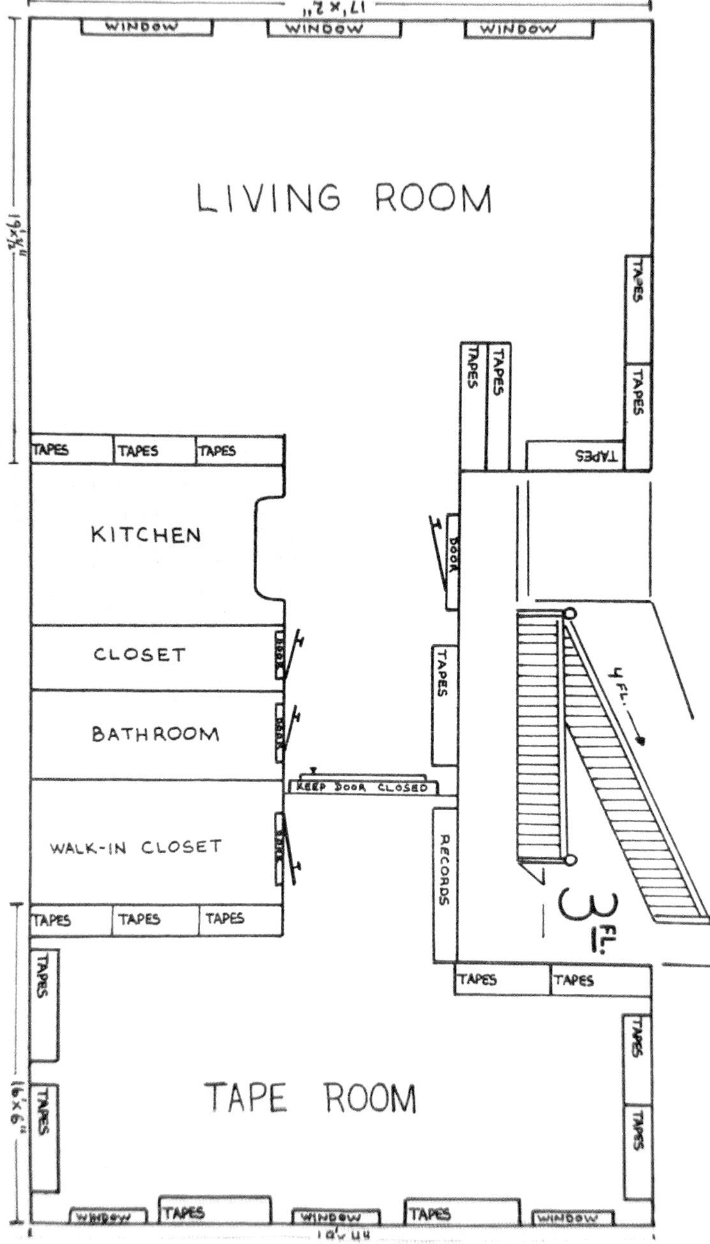

WINDOW
WINDOW
WINDOW
LIVING ROOM
TAPES
TAPES
TAPES
TAPES
TAPES
TAPES
TAPES
TAPES
KITCHEN
DOOR
CLOSET
TAPES
4 FL.
BATHROOM
KEEP DOOR CLOSED
WALK-IN CLOSET
RECORDS
3 FL.
TAPES
TAPES
TAPES
TAPES
TAPES
TAPES
TAPES
TAPES
TAPE ROOM
TAPES
WINDOW
TAPES
WINDOW
TAPES
WINDOW

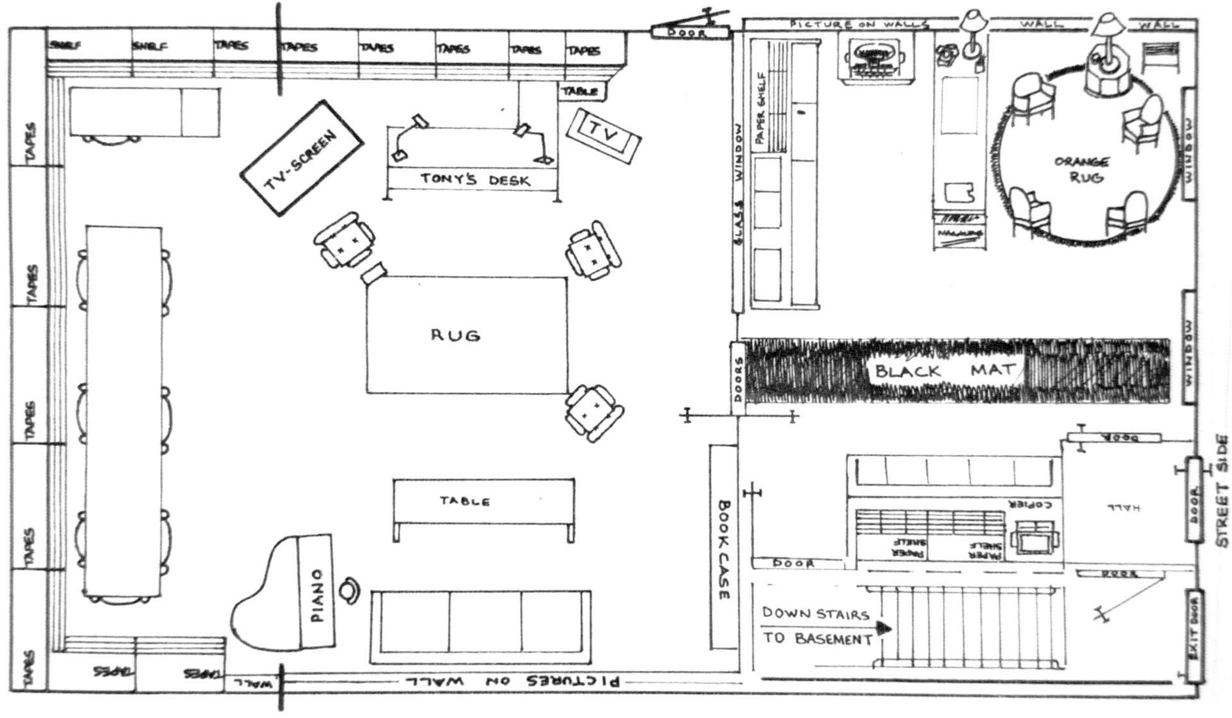
SHELF
SHELF
TAPES
TAPES
TAPES
TAPES
TAPES
TAPES
DOOR
PICTURE ON WALLS
WALL
WALL
TABLE
TV
TV-SCREEN
TONY'S DESK
PAPER SHELF
GLASS WINDOW
ORANGE RUG
WINDOW
TAPES
TAPES
TAPES
TAPES
TAPES
RUG
DOORS
BLACK MAT
WINDOW
DOOR
TABLE
COPIER
HALL
PAPER SHELF
PAPER SHELF
BOOK CASE
DOOR
DOOR
STREET SIDE
DOOR
PIANO
DOWN STAIRS
TO BASEMENT
EXIT DOOR
TAPES
TAPES
WALL
PICTURES ON WALL

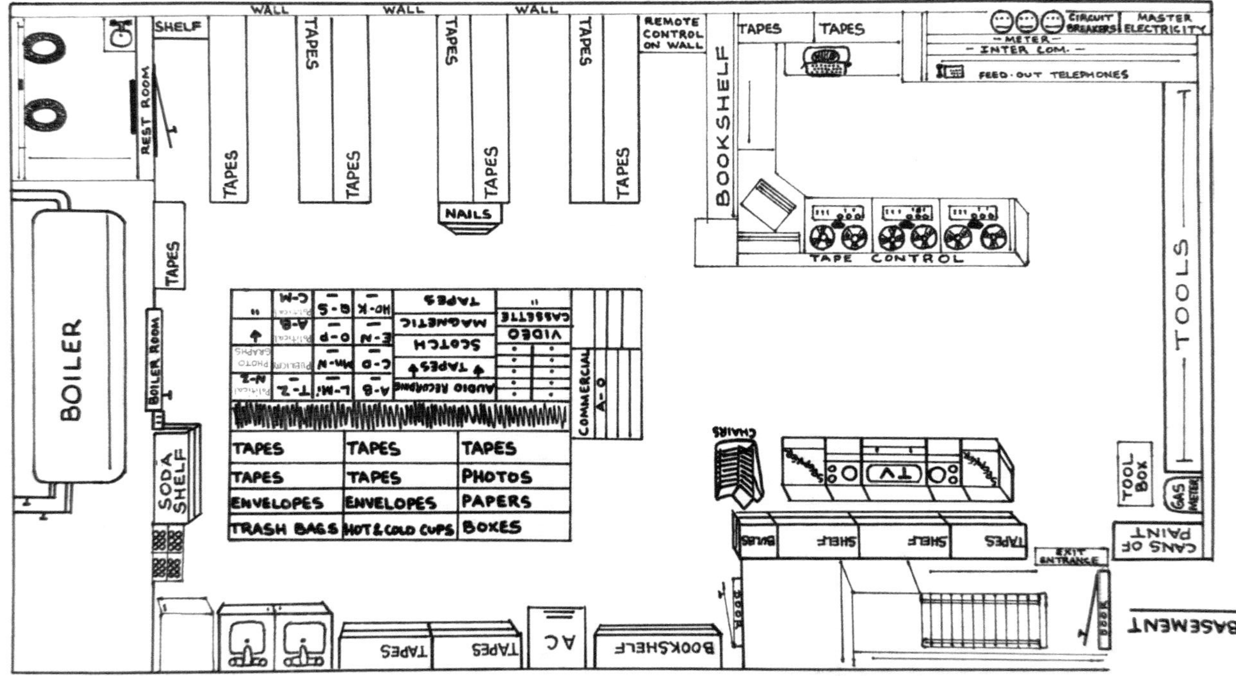
BASEMENT
BOILER
REST ROOM
BOILER ROOM
SODA SHELF
SHELF
WALL
TAPES
NAILS
REMOTE CONTROL ON WALL
BOOKSHELF
TAPE CONTROL
CIRCUIT BREAKERS
MASTER ELECTRICITY
METER
INTER COM.
FEED-OUT TELEPHONES
TOOLS
TOOL BOX
GAS METER
CANS OF PAINT
EXIT ENTRANCE
DOOR
CHAIRS
TV
BULBS
SHELF
AC
BOOKSHELF
TAPES
PHOTOS
ENVELOPES
PAPERS
TRASH BAGS
HOT & COLD CUPS
BOXES
AUDIO RECORDING
TAPES
SCOTCH
MAGNETIC
VIDEO
CASSETTE
COMMERCIAL
A-O
A-B
C-D
E-N
HO-K
L-Mi
Mn-N
O-P
Q-S
T-Z
Political A-B
Political C-M
Political N-Z
PUBLIC
PHOTO GRAPHS

RP-72-R WNYC INVISIBLE FRIENDS

7:03 10/22/63

A world we hardly know. Jackie, a young girl, says; "Your stepping on my shadow." She has an invisible donkey with a broken back. Her mother speaks about Jackie's invisible friend, Baby Bear. Jackie's brother and sister also have colorful imaginations. A neighbor speaks about her kid's colorful imaginations; invisible friends, horses, and pen-pals. Ghosty is one of the names.

RP-193-R WNYC INTERVIEW WITH EDWARD STEICHEN

7:13 3/3/64

The Museum of Modern Art is going to open the Edward Steichen Photography Center. The first exhibition is the "Photographer's Eye." Edward Steichen is becoming interested in sound. He wants to add sound to his film, "The Life of A Tree." He talks at length about the sounds that he wants to record and sound in general.

I

Ice Skating
"If You're Good You'll Go to Heaven"
I Have Three Heads
Industrial and Educational Uses of Cassette Tapes
Infant Vocalization
In Relation to Shoes, Late 1960s
Inside the Butcher's Ice Box
Intercommunication
Interview About Banks
Interview About the Contrasting Roles of Women and Men in Childrearing; Material for an Ultralife Battery Commercial; Material for an Ad Promoting Carbon Monoxide Detectors
Interview with Edward Steichen
Interview with Italian man; Recording Test
Interview with Nurse Joanne Lamb [About] Organ Donors
Interview with Puerto Ricans About Their Immigration to the United States
Interview with Rabbi Jack Bemporad
Interviews with Record Collectors
Interview with Unidentified Man
Invisible Friends, 1963
Irish Mouth Music
Italian Street Festival
It's a Boy

RP-50-R WNYC JIMMY GIUFFRE - GM LOBBY

4:47 5/17/66

Recording studios are made for silence, not sound. They started because recording machines were not portable, so recording technicians needed a place nearby to make their recordings. Today's portable recorder can go almost anywhere. Tony Schwartz and Jimmy Giuffre go to the Lobby of the GM building on fifty-seventh street because of the beautiful reverb. Jimmy plays his stuff.

J

James Fassett on His Life and Composition "Symphony of the Birds"
Japanese Flute Recording from Pete Seeger
Jean Ritchie & Hally Wood
Jewish Song; Sculptor Hammering
Jimmy Giuffre at the Guggenheim Museum, New York, New York, 1973-08-23
Jimmy Giuffre at the Whitney Museum, New York, New York, 1968-04-23
Jimmy Giuffre Clarinet Improvisations against Various Live and Taped Sounds, [1961?]-05-30
Jimmy Giuffre Discussion on the Effects of Dental Work on Clarinet Playing, 1961-09
Jimmy Giuffre Performing in the Lobby of the GM Building New York, N.Y.
Joan of Arc Art Class
John Cage Performing *Atlas Eclipticalis*
John Dowland—First Book of Ayres—Marshall McLuhan
John Lee Hooker
John Henry
Jonathan, Tony, Reenah, and Larry Schwartz Talk and Sing, 1962-05
Jugoslav Chorus
Jump Rope
Jungles of Memory

RP-289-R WNYC LAUGHTER

8:06 4/2/63

On television we hear a lot of laughter during situation comedies. The laughter comes from "vines" of tape stored in the recording studio. This is National Laughter Week so we listen to the history of recorded laughter; canned laughter, cued laughter, contageous laughter, spontaneous laughter, and the real laughter of children, Italian women, friends, and theater audiences.

RP-343-R WNYC LONG HAIR AND LEARNING

3:32 2/6/68

Over the last few years men have been growing their hair longer and longer. High-school students have started to do the same. School principals have their own view of the situation. Teenagers talk about long hair and education.They guess at Tony's attitude on the subject.

K

Kayla Dance Tape, 1982-10-15
Kayla [Schwartz] Interrupting Tony, 1966-02-06
Kayla [Schwartz], Broken Leg
Ken & Wendy Heyman's Wedding, 1960-09-11
Kids and Cats
Kids Singing "Jingle Bells"
Kids Street Games
Kitchen Sounds
Kitten Purring
Klezmer Music
Knife Pitchman and Jewelry Pitchman at Auction
Koch, Ed, "ah's," 1986-09-01

L

Laughter
Lavoris
LBJ & dogs, 1972-09
Leading + Misleading Sound
Learning a Language
Lincoln Square Community
Listening Game #1
Live Broadcasts after Robert Kennedy's Assassination, 1968
Long Hair, Dalton Kids, 1966-09-20
Longitude 41 (take 3)
Louis Spiegler Cello Audition
Lower East Side
Lullabies #1
Luncheon Keynote: A Personal Revelation

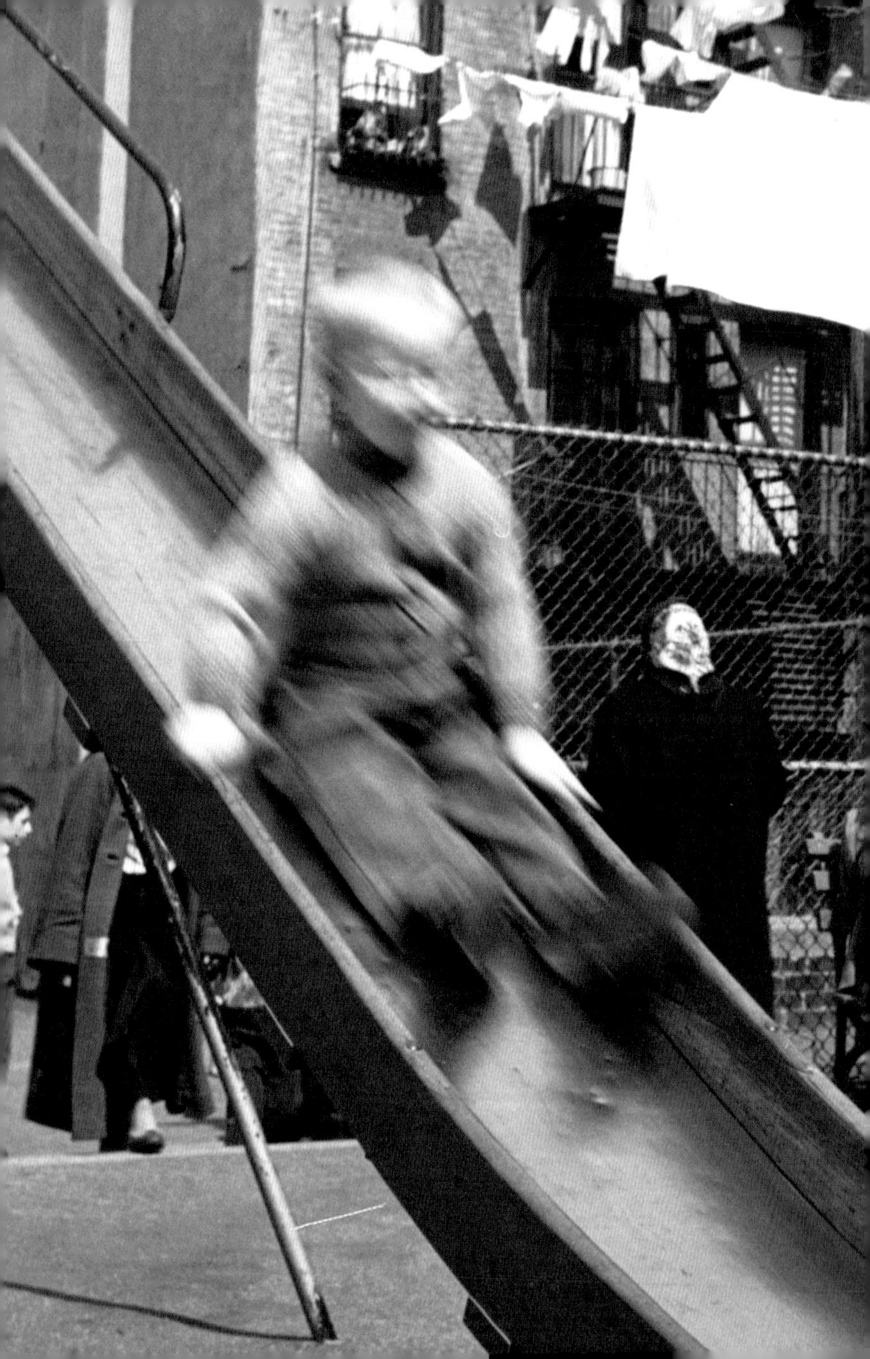

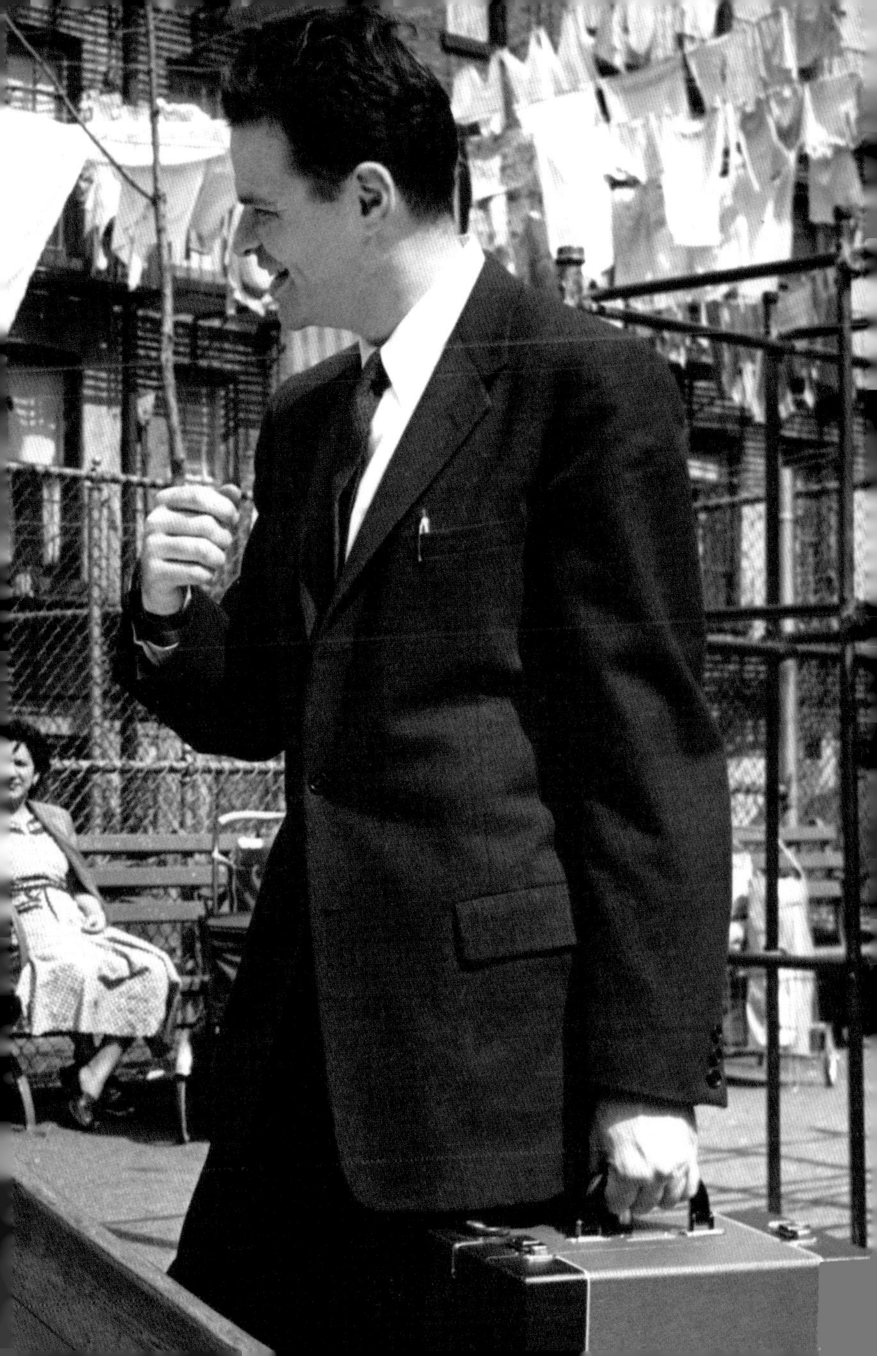

RP-88-R WNYC MORNING PEOPLE

3:27 5/13/69

There are two types of people; night people and morning people. On his early morning walks Tony meets morning people; a sanitation truck, a central park painter who polishes furniture for a living, and a blind man who sees the world through the tap of his cane.

M

Machinery Sounds
Macy's Fireworks
Man Talks About Being Alone on the Streets
Dr. Margaret Mead
Marshall McLuhan and Tony Schwartz Phone Calls 1977-07-21 and 1978-06-10
Mary Lou Williams
Mary Travers in Washington Square
Material for Ernie Kovacs's show, August 1955
Mayfair Theater Barker
Memory, Con-Ed, Meter Reader
Message Repeater Machines
Milk Dating
Moe Asch Interview, 1971-03-11
Molded Shoe Casting, 1964-03-11
Mom & Pop Stores
Moondog
Moon People
Morning People
Mothers Calling Children
Muhammad Ali on Voter Registration
Murray Lerner, 1961-04-27
Musical Instruments: Unusual & Foreign
Musical Selections for Sunlamp Timing
Music & Foods of National Groups in New York City
Music Boxes
Music Happenings #1
Musician Who Isn't a Musician
Music in the Rain
Music, Old Rundown Piano

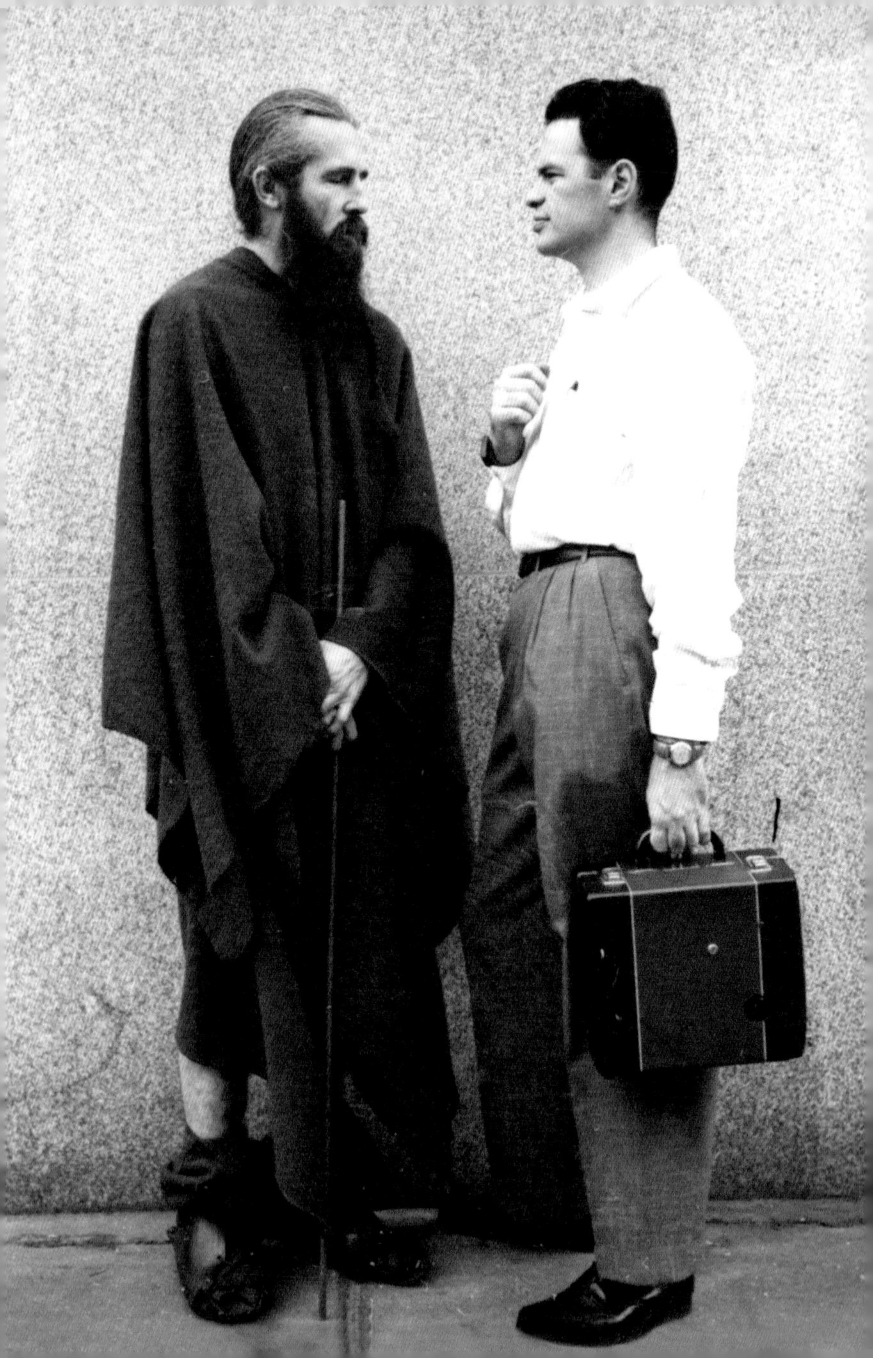

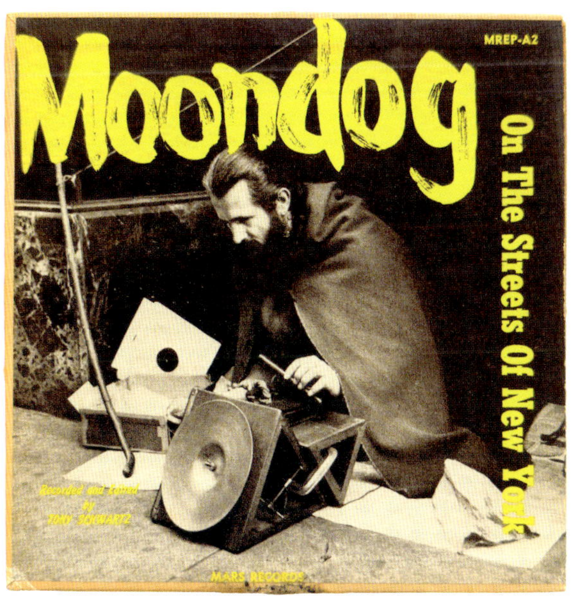

Tony Schwartz with Moondog, ca. 1953

RP-363-R WNYC NUMBERS

6:27

Tony was in a place where people say numbers; in an elevator. Numbers play an important role in our lives. They can be used by a little girl singing "Two, four, six, eight,....", in a grocery store, for an appointment, for telling time or temperature, in a gym, at an auction, by a woman selling flowers, by kids playing football, by hockey players, for firing a rocket, in music, in a factory, for pleasure or business, in mathematics, by a computor warming up, and for making a date.

N

Nagra, 1973-05
Naming of Dogs
Nancy Grows Up
Narrowcasting
Nathaniel Stern, Queer Rights
National Civil Rights Museum, Presentation and Comments, 1996-09-27
New Morning Cereals, Telephone Discussion, 1989-10-30
News About Food Prices
News of the Atom Bomb
New York Doctor Telephone Service
New York in Hi-Fi
Night, 1963-02
Nixon on Watergate, Coke Commercial
No. 1, Loud
Non-Commercials
None of the Above
Norwegian String Band
Number You Have Reached Has Been Changed
N.Y. Enthusiasts, 1979-04-07
NYU Students' Questions About Sound, 1960s

New York 19

Conceived, recorded, edited and narrated by **TONY SCHWARTZ**

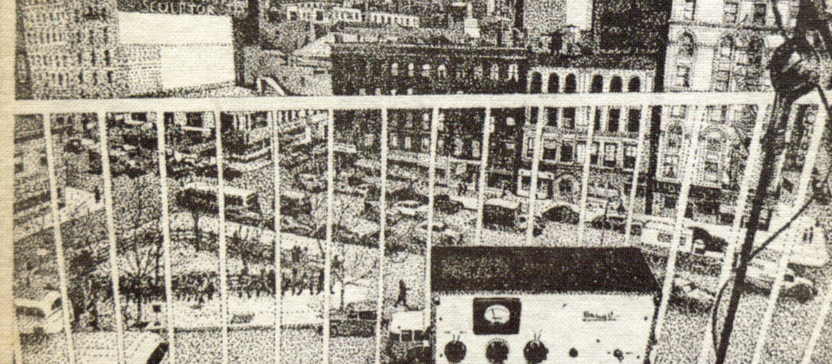

FP 58 FOLKWAYS RECORDS & SERVICE CORP., N. Y. **FP 58**

MUSIC OF THE STREETS

Nat Hentoff

THE REPORTER, OCTOBER 1, 1959

It is the contention of Tony Schwartz, a thirty-six-year-old New Yorker for whom a tape recorder is a constant third ear, that there is much more music in the streets than we realize.

In *New York 19* (Folkways), Schwartz has focused on a study of "the folklore of the community in which I live." Postal Zone 19 in New York is bounded by Sixtieth Street on the north, Forty-eighth Street on the south, the Hudson on the west, and Fifth Avenue and the Rockefeller Center enclave on the east.

Among the music makers he has collected therein are street players, theater barkers, pen criers (". . . you can go downtown, uptown, into town, in the summertime, in the wintertime . . . All the way through, you'll never get a pen like this . . . You can write Yiddish, English . . . You can print; you can sketch with this very same pen."), children, street preachers, a Puerto Rican religious service, a molten African American gospel tune, and several other daily local music events that are not covered by the New York *Times* or *Musical America*.

Schwartz's biggest success to date is *1,2,3 and a Zing Zing Zing* (Folkways), subtitled "Street Games and Songs of the Children of New York City." In it he recorded African American, Puerto Rican, Jewish, Irish, and other children in an area two blocks wide and twenty blocks long in west midtown Manhattan. "In the folk process," Schwartz explains in his notes for the set, "songs are generally passed along from adult to child. In street games and songs, the process differs; they are passed from child to child."

There's a dithyrambic section, "Rhythm," that "was recorded in the basement of a housing-project apartment building." African American and Puerto Rican teen-agers accompany their singing with "one bongo drum, several chairs, a long wide wooden bench, metal waste baskets, several sticks, a hair comb covered with tissue paper and an empty Pepsi-Cola bottle." The album also contains some of the most naturally flowing singing ever recorded—a twelve-year-old girl leading a group of children in songs she'd learned at Fresh Air Fund camps.

A more detailed sound sketch by Schwartz of urban "folk" speech rhythms is *The New York Taxi Driver* ("Spontaneous, in-the-cab recordings of actual New York City cab drivers," Columbia). "Now if I go home and give her a good day's pay," one driver describes his union, "she's happy. She's happy, I'm happy. Avoid all trouble. She's got the kids ready to say as soon as I come in the house, 'How much did you make today, Daddy?' Out in the street, they'll call out, 'Daddy, how much did you make today?' 'Shut up, will ya, do you want everyone to know my business?'"

Schwartz was trained as a commercial artist. His now full-time involvement in "sound hunting" began in 1946 when he bought a wire recorder to make off-the-air recordings of folk-music broadcasts. Gradually the avocation took up more and more of his time, and now, besides creating albums, Schwartz does sound tracks for films and TV shows, radio and

TV commercials based on street speech and attitudes, radio programs, and even an occasional night-club turn with his tape machines at the Baq Room on Sixth Avenue between Fifty-fifth and Fifty-sixth Streets.

Schwartz's WNYC radio program *Sounds of My City* (Folkways) won the first-place Prix Italia in the World Radio Festival at Rimini three years ago. He had originally prepared a version of the program for CBS, which had balked at paying the $2,000 initiation fee for the festival. When WNYC finally entered the program, the cost was assumed by the National Association of Educational Broadcasters.

The album, like several other Schwartz collections (most notably *Music in the Streets* and *Millions of Musicians*, Folkways), is a startling reminder of the uniqueness of the familiar. There are sounds of ships, shoeshine boys, the staccato matter-of-factness of doormen at strip joints, and the vigorously diversified music and speech textures of the language groups within the city. A particularly vivid skein of examples is made up of a Jewish Friday-night religious service at home, a jaunty Italian saint's-day parade, a vibrant Puerto Rican store-front church service; and an eighteenth-century hymn, "Joy to the World," transformed by a Harlem choir a week before Christmas into a much clearer illustration of where the indigenous Afro-American beat in jazz came from than any jazz history book offers.

The same *Sounds of My City*, which is composed in large part of excerpts from other Schwartz albums, also has caught such city sounds as politicians and their sound trucks ("My opponent has no program. His ten years of inactivity, unavailability, and futility have *demonstrated* that he has no program"); spitting, wailing cats at three in the morning; and the buoyantly unself-conscious play speech of a fourteen-month-old.

. . .

It was Schwartz who made the first recorded documentary of the Puerto Rican experience in New York (*Nueva York*, Folkways). The project, begun in 1948, took eight years and is a painfully evocative self-portrait of the emigrants. A mordant juke-box record, "A Puerto Rican Peasant in New York," is played as a Puerto Rican translates the lyrics into English. The languid background guitars contrast ironically with the determined words: "I am going back to Puerto Rico even if I have to go back swimming. There, even just eating bananas, I will go through life singing."

Schwartz includes a West Side woman's comments on the "filth and misery" of the Puerto Ricans on the streets between West End Avenue and Riverside Drive. ("I wish they hadn't come here in the first place. They aren't welcome.") For counterpoint, there are stories by Puerto Ricans of hostile engagements with landlords and the oppressive apartments once they get them. There's a Puerto Rican teen-ager who says: "They come by and watch us dancing out in the street and they think it's terrible and disgusting; but you know, they do the same thing too, only in night clubs."

Nueva York contains Puerto Rican children learning English by telling the story of Little Red Riding Hood ("You have a big eyes . . . you have a big mouth . . . O.K., my mother, I come for take a lunch to you . . . The family sit in the bed and eat good fruit"), along with a teacher's reaction ("We find it difficult to teach children who are hungry . . . the special class *is* to teach them English, but before you can teach them English, you've got to make them warm and comfortable").

Schwartz has several works in progress: an album on the folklore of foods, involving sound expeditions to foreign restaurants;

a study of a pawnshop and its clients; a survey of superstitions; an investigation of what children think about their teachers; and an album of people's reactions to radio and TV. He has also recorded for Vanguard *The Sound of Children*, a series of conversations among children.

"The average album I make," says Schwartz, "takes about five years. Some have required only one year and others take as much as nine." He has also done a boxing documentary that was originally commissioned by a major label, "but they felt it was too sad. They wanted more of the glory of it all and couldn't stand the tragedy."

Schwartz works with a Nagra, a Swiss tape recorder that weighs sixteen pounds. He carries it nearly all the time, since he never knows when he'll hear a city sound he wants to file. "The best recordings I've done," Schwartz notes, "are those I've made openly. If you can establish a relationship with the people you record, you can have a ton of equipment and they won't feel self-conscious. Sure, I suppose you can call what I do 'candid' recordings, but by 'candid' I mean frank, not hidden."

Nat Hentoff (1925–2017) was a peerless culture and politics columnist for *The Village Voice* and many other publications, a venerated music critic and liner note writer who was named an NEA Jazz Master, and a tireless advocate for the First Amendment and humanitarian causes.

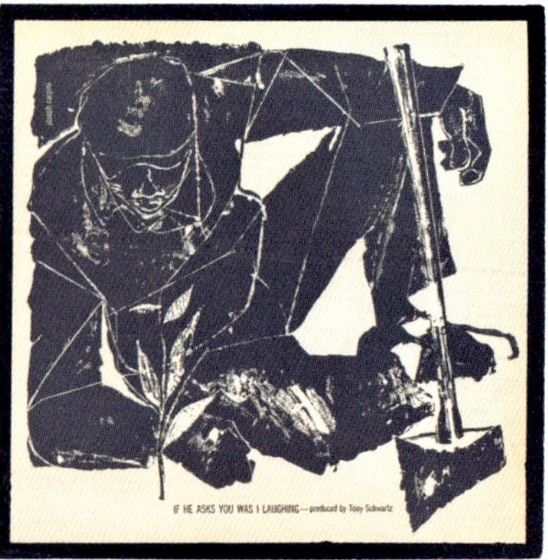
IF HE ASKS YOU WAS I LAUGHING— produced by Tony Schwartz

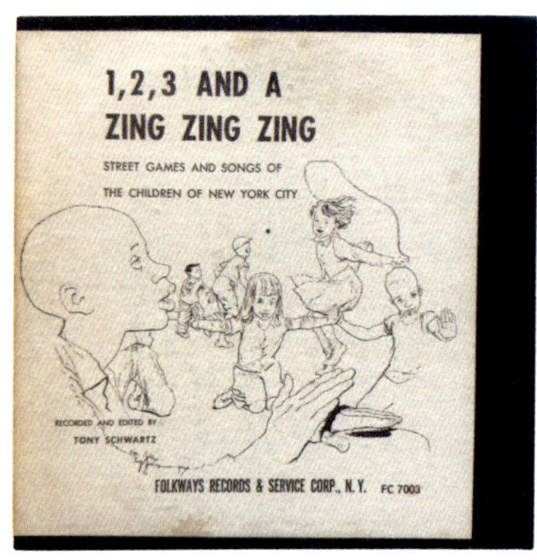
1,2,3 AND A
ZING ZING ZING
STREET GAMES AND SONGS OF
THE CHILDREN OF NEW YORK CITY
RECORDED AND EDITED BY
TONY SCHWARTZ
FOLKWAYS RECORDS & SERVICE CORP., N.Y. FC 7003

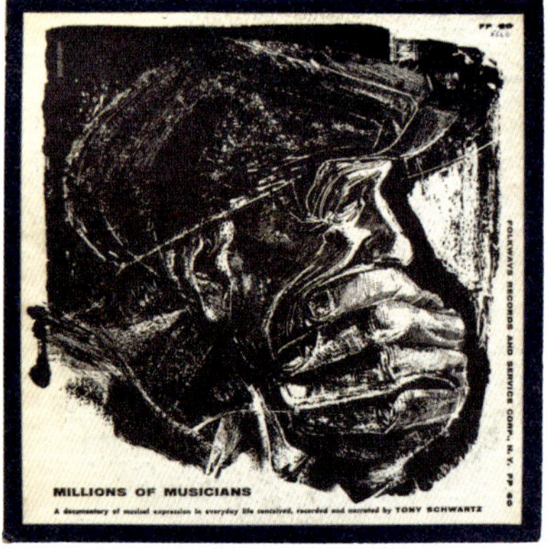
FP 60
FOLKWAYS RECORDS AND SERVICE CORP., N.Y. FP 60
MILLIONS OF MUSICIANS
A documentary of musical expression in everyday life conceived, recorded and narrated by TONY SCHWARTZ

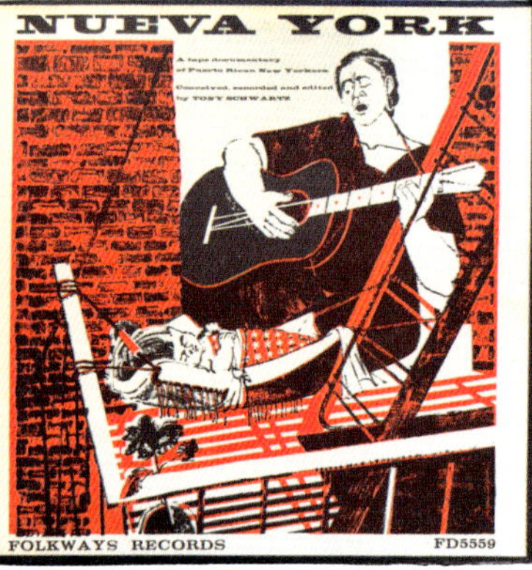
NUEVA YORK
FOLKWAYS RECORDS
FD5559

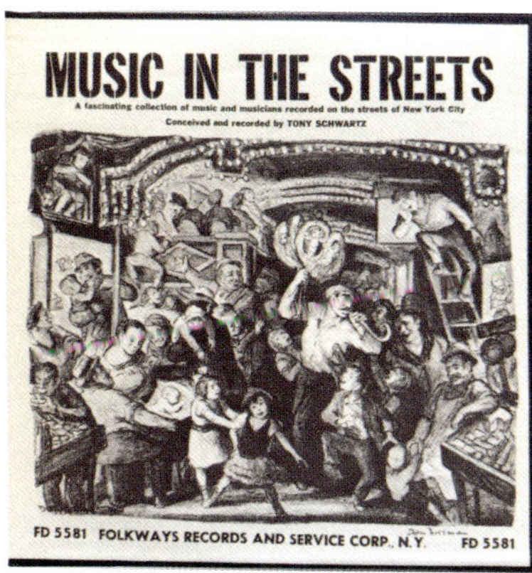
MUSIC IN THE STREETS
A fascinating collection of music and musicians recorded on the streets of New York City
Conceived and recorded by TONY SCHWARTZ
FD 5581 FOLKWAYS RECORDS AND SERVICE CORP., N.Y. FD 5581

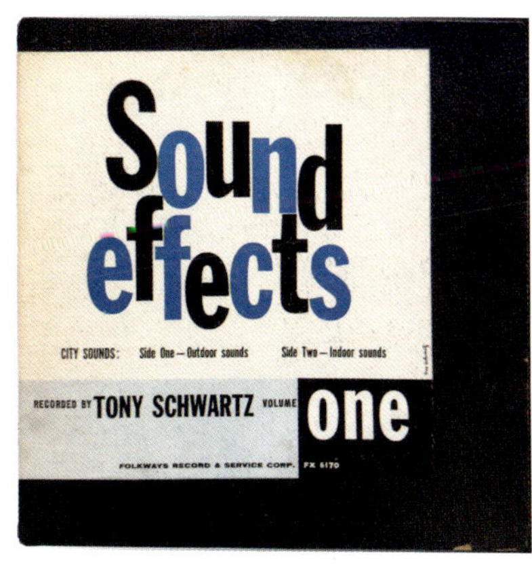
Sound effects
CITY SOUNDS: Side One – Outdoor sounds Side Two – Indoor sounds
RECORDED BY TONY SCHWARTZ VOLUME one
FOLKWAYS RECORD & SERVICE CORP. FX 6170

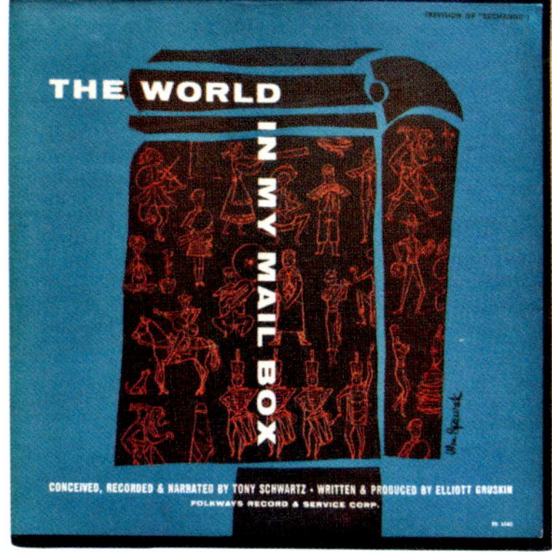
THE WORLD IN MY MAIL BOX
CONCEIVED, RECORDED & NARRATED BY TONY SCHWARTZ · WRITTEN & PRODUCED BY ELLIOTT GRUSKIN
FOLKWAYS RECORD & SERVICE CORP.

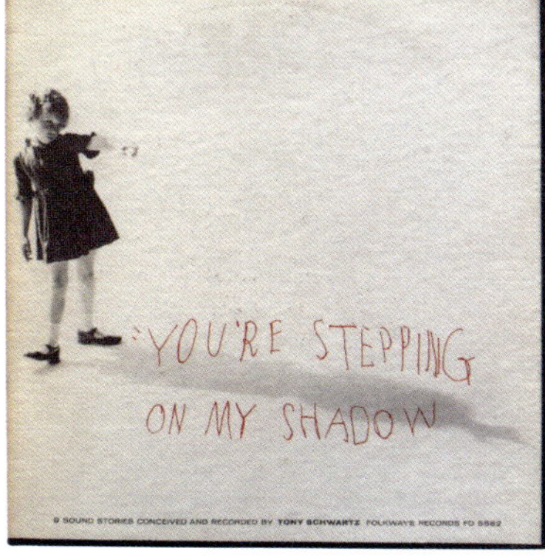
YOU'RE STEPPING
ON MY SHADOW
9 SOUND STORIES CONCEIVED AND RECORDED BY TONY SCHWARTZ FOLKWAYS RECORDS FD 5562

RP-163-R WNYC OUT OUR WINDOW

6:19 3/26/63

Windows are opened in the spring. Teenagers play baseball in front of the house. Other sounds heard from the window include; Mrs. Klein hanging out her wash, birds chirping at 7:00 AM, the garbage being collected, street jackhammers, building construction, an air-raid drill, church bells, a marching band, kids playing football in the street, a street gospel group, the pitter-patter of rain, a street musician, politicians in their sound trucks, and screeching cats at 3:00 AM.

O

Ocean & Water Sounds #1
Office Sounds, 1961
Old Age: Shoeshine Men
Old Record Players, Cylinders
Old Records (78's), 1967-04
Old Time Radio
Old Woman on Cat
One Breath
On Play: Adults and Children Describing How to Play Games
On Schools without Walls
On Smoking
The Opera and the Baby
Orchard Street Calls
Orson Welles, Commercial Recording Session
Other Guy Ken
Outdoor Furniture Generic
Outdoor Sound in N.Y.
Out Our Window
Outtake Auto-Sounds

RP-44-R WNYC PERPETUAL MOTION

2:02 6/18/68

Interview with house plumber whose hobby is to search for perpetual motion. A track in a film is described as perpetual motion in sound. The beep tone seems to be able to go higher and lower ad infinitum.

RP-79-R WNYC THE POSTMAN

4:43 12/8/64

The mailman sorts some mail in Tony's house. In an interview he says that he puts his mind to his work. He leaves for work at 4:30, starts at 6:00, boxes up the mail, and finishes at 2:30 pm. Most people are nice to him.

P

Parents of Tommy Niremberg
Parkway Restaurant Music, 1975-03-08
Part of a Passover Seder Meal; Grandfather and Grandson Talking About Exodus out of Egypt
Party: Birthday & Surprise, Teenage, 1972–1973
Party (Dream Whip), 1964-11
Pat Connell and His Father Discuss Life, 1966-10-05
Paul from Pool Singing, 1983-03-07
Paul Robeson on Sholem Aleichem
Paul Sorvino, Takes, 1960s
Peddlers' Chants (Early American)
Pentax Sounds
People #2
Perpetual Motion
Pet Milk Advertisements with Pat Connell, 1964-06-09
Phone Conversation with Carl Sagan
Picket Lines
Pittsburgh Yiddish Songs
Plumber Harry Goldstein Describes a Family Funeral
The Postman
Presearch
Presidents #2, 1960
Private Languages
Progressive Party Convention 7/24/48

Q

Quit that Smokin', Joseph Jenkins, Roberts Paideia Academy, Cincinnati, OH

RP-10-R WNYC RESTORED EARSIGHT

1:55 3/31/70

Mr. Olsen regains his hearing after an operation. He is especially excited about hearing the sounds of rustling sheets, walking on a carpet, the wind, a dripping faucet, and the crinkling of a page in a book.

RP-122-R WNYC RESTURANT MUSIC

5:51 2/2/65

Restaurant sounds and music. A musical menu means different tunes for different tastes; a German restaurant, a Hawian restaurant, a Russian restaurant, an American meat restaurant, etc.

R

Radio Commercial for Butter, 1976-06
Radios Keep Me Company
Radios, Portable, Early 1970s
Rain + Thunder and "Jazz" Whistling, Early 1960s and Early 1970s
Rain, Early 1970s
Ralph Nader on Air Bags, 1980-07
RCA Building Guides
Reading at "Double" then Normal Speed
Recording of a Faulty Machine
Recording of Unidentified Pianist with Metronome
Recordings of Auto Interiors
Reenah and Thief, 1990-11-26
Rembrandt Painting
Restaurants #2, 1971-09
Restored Earsight
Rev. Kelsey and His Congregation, Frank Warner, Woody Guthrie, and Dave Macon, 1952
Ritz Cafe, Discount, 1987-07-01
Riverside Hospital Bongo
Rocks & Gravel, 1967-01-03
Roofers, Late 1960s
Room Tone, 1962-06
Roosevelt Hospital Emergency Ward, 1954-03-30
Roosevelt Raceway, 1964-03-05
Rough Material #19
Ruth Rubin on Snow

RP-237-R WNYC SHORT ORDER TALK

4:05 2/1/66

Many resturants in New York have waiters and menus that are impossible to understand. The short-order field has its own language. A "burn" is a chocolate float. A "draw" is a cup of coffee. "Hold the grass" means no lettuce. "Check the ice!" means that a beautiful woman just walked in.

S

Saint Patrick's Parade
Same Voice 12 Years Apart
Sanitation Ticket, 1982
Santa Claus, 1960s
Schoolbus Riddles
Selling a Used Car in New York City
Sessions at a Marriage Counselor
Seventeen Anti-Smoking Radio Spots
Seven Valium Radio Spots, 1984-10-29
Shift Break, 5-1-58
Shoe Repair Shop Ads
Short Conversation About a Strange Pronunciation
Shortcut thru New York, 1974-03
Short Order Talk
Shower, Shampoo, and Singing Sounds [ca. mid-1960s]
Singer's Warm Up
Singing in School
SNCC #2, 1960s
Snow Cars & Shoveling, ca. 1957–63
Snow Street Sounds, 1950s–60s
Soda Pouring and Drinking after Work, 1960s
Sonar, 1960s
Song About a Bus
Songs Sung by a Woman About Her Walk-up Flat and Past Happiness
Songs without Words
Sonny Terry Performs Harmonica Breakdown
Sound of Timepieces
Sound Pollution, 1960s

Sounds from Inside Nathan's Hot Dogs on Coney Island, 1965-03
Sounds from New York, 1961-07-30, Yma Sumac
Sounds of a Department Store Elevator
Sounds of Al Braverman's Pawn Shop
Sounds of Bowling
Sounds of Commuter Trains + Office Sounds, 1960s and 1970s
Sounds of Hands
Spanish Children from the Amsterdam Housing Project, 63rd and 10th
Speech Patterns: Sal De Grazia, Speaking Backwards
Speeded Up Speech
Speeds of Sound
Stage Delicatessen, 1965-03
Stella Adler : History of Yiddish Theater
Store Sounds, New York City, Late 1950s–Early 1960s
Subway Singing

RP-167-R WNYC SOUNDS OF YESTERYEAR

3:41 8/24/65

The Huntington-Hartford exhibition for the 50th anniversary of the Woman's City Club of New York, includes a selection of sounds not heard anymore; the coal being delivered, the 9th Avenue "L", the man buying old clothes or selling vegetables, the water dripping into the refrigerator pan, the old horse and wagon, the early automobile and its horns.

RP-166-R WNYC SOUND OF TIMEPIECES

5:52 6/2/64

The sounds of time-pieces; the silence of a sun-dial, birds chirping, the thunder of a storm that halts sun-dial time-keeping, a rooster heralding the dawn, a ticking grandfather clock with chimes, a grandfather's watch, an old clock, a quiet alarm clock, a clock speeding up, the soft ticking of a new watch, and an electronic watch with a humming tuning fork.

RP-139-R WNYC SOUND POLLUTION

9:09 3/28/67

Two types of air pollution; physical particles that fill the air, and sound or noise that moves the air. Noise from the city; traffic horns, sirens, street hammers, cement mixers, motor-cyles, etc.

Sound verses noise; an emotional distinction: The sound of a fire-engine is noise when you are trying to go to sleep but is a welcome sound when your house is burning down. Time can effect ones perception of sound; water dripping, electronically reproduced. Technology brings new sounds and noise; helicopters flying over a community. The delivery of newspaper rolls keeps a neighbor awake all night. He speaks about the problem as we listen to the disturbing sounds. A lot of people have to get together to take effective action against unwanted sound.

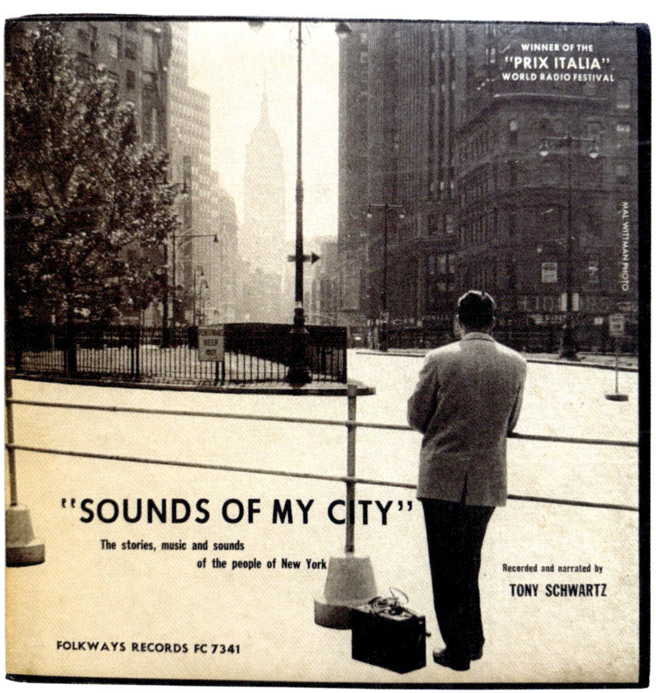
WINNER OF THE
"PRIX ITALIA"
WORLD RADIO FESTIVAL
MAL WITTMAN PHOTO
"SOUNDS OF MY CITY"
The stories, music and sounds
of the people of New York
Recorded and narrated by
TONY SCHWARTZ
FOLKWAYS RECORDS FC 7341

49 Vernon Park,
Clontarf,
Dublin,
Ireland.
Dec. 4th 1957.

Seymour N. Siegal Esq.,
Director,
Station W.N.Y.C.
New York 7, N.Y.

Dear Sir,

Some time ago - last April to be exact - I heard a feature, entitled "Sounds of My City" by Tony Schwartz (Italian Press Association Prize 1956), from Radio Eireann in Dublin.

New York is a place I have always longed to see - and on my present wage I know I never will, unless I win a fortune. But the night I heard that feature I was carried there in spirit - I just closed my eyes in Dublin and opened my ears in New York - it was all I had ever imagined your city would sound like - and more.

So I thought if I could buy that record I could close my eyes and "visit" New York whenever I felt like doing so. I searched all over Dublin but no store could help me. Eventually I wrote to Radio Eireann and they suggested that *you* might be able to end my search, but they warned me that copying and copyright fees might be expensive.

49 Vernon Park,
Clontarf, Dublin, Ireland.
Dec. 4th 1957.

Seymour N. Siegal Esq.,
Director,
Station W.N.Y.C.
New York 7, N.Y.

Dear Sir,

Some time ago—last April to be exact—I heard a feature, entitled "Sounds of My City" by Tony Schwartz (Italian Press Association Prize 1956), from Radio Eireann in Dublin.

New York is a place I have always longed to see—and on my present wage I know I never will, unless I win a fortune. But the night I heard that feature I was carried there in spirit—I just closed my eyes in Dublin and opened my ears in New York—it was all I had ever imagined your city would sound like—and more.

So I thought if I could buy that record I could close my eyes and "visit" New York whenever I felt like doing so. I searched all over Dublin but no store could help me. Eventually I wrote to Radio Eireann and they suggested that you might be able to end my search, but they warned me that copying and copyright fees might be expensive.

I would obliged therefore if you could tell me if the feature is obtainable commercially as a record (L.P. or E.P. or otherwise) and, if so obtainable the title under which it is produced, the record company releasing it and it's catalogue number. If it is not obtainable in the ordinary record stores can you advise me where I might buy a copy and also its price. I could not afford expensive copying and copyright fees. I definitely assure you that it will not be used for public performance.

Your sympathetic consideration of my request would much oblige. I sincerely hope you may see your way to helping me.

Yours faithfully,
Richard M. Butler

T

Taking a Doll to the Park
Talking Toys
Taxi Drivers—Comments
Teenage Guitarists
Teenagers and Mandolins
Telephone Calls to Various Operators
Test of Radio Shack vs. Sony Recorder
Thoughts on Automation
Tony & Reenah—Wedding
Tony Kraber Sings Several Versions of Doodle Doodle Dandy
Tony Schwartz and Others Talk About Con-Edison, ca. 1965
Tony Schwartz Answering Machine Outgoing Message, Version 4
Tony Schwartz Discusses His Agoraphobia with an Unidentified Man
Tony Schwartz, Dreams, 1966-03-06 and 1966-04-04
Tony Schwartz Interviews Man Who Lost His Job, 1990-08-18
Tony Schwartz Phone Call to AT&T Language Line Interpreter Services
Tony Schwartz Presents Interviews and Comments on Permanent Press Clothing
Tony Schwartz Presents the Sound of Coins Dropping on Metal and a Table
Tony's Experience with Handshaking, 1986-07-01
Traffic Noises on 42nd Street

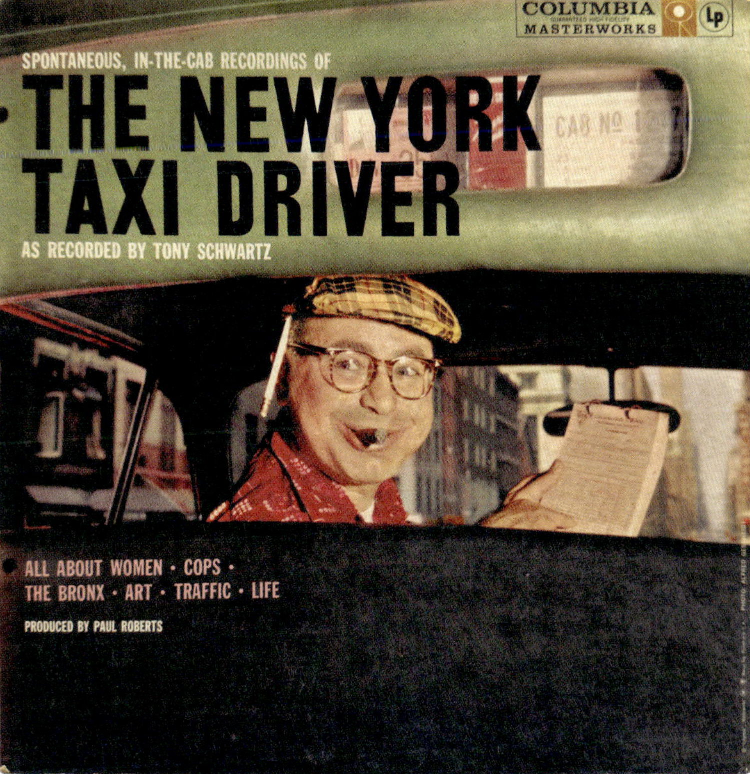
COLUMBIA
GUARANTEED HIGH FIDELITY
MASTERWORKS
LP
SPONTANEOUS, IN-THE-CAB RECORDINGS OF
THE NEW YORK
TAXI DRIVER
AS RECORDED BY TONY SCHWARTZ
ALL ABOUT WOMEN · COPS ·
THE BRONX · ART · TRAFFIC · LIFE
PRODUCED BY PAUL ROBERTS

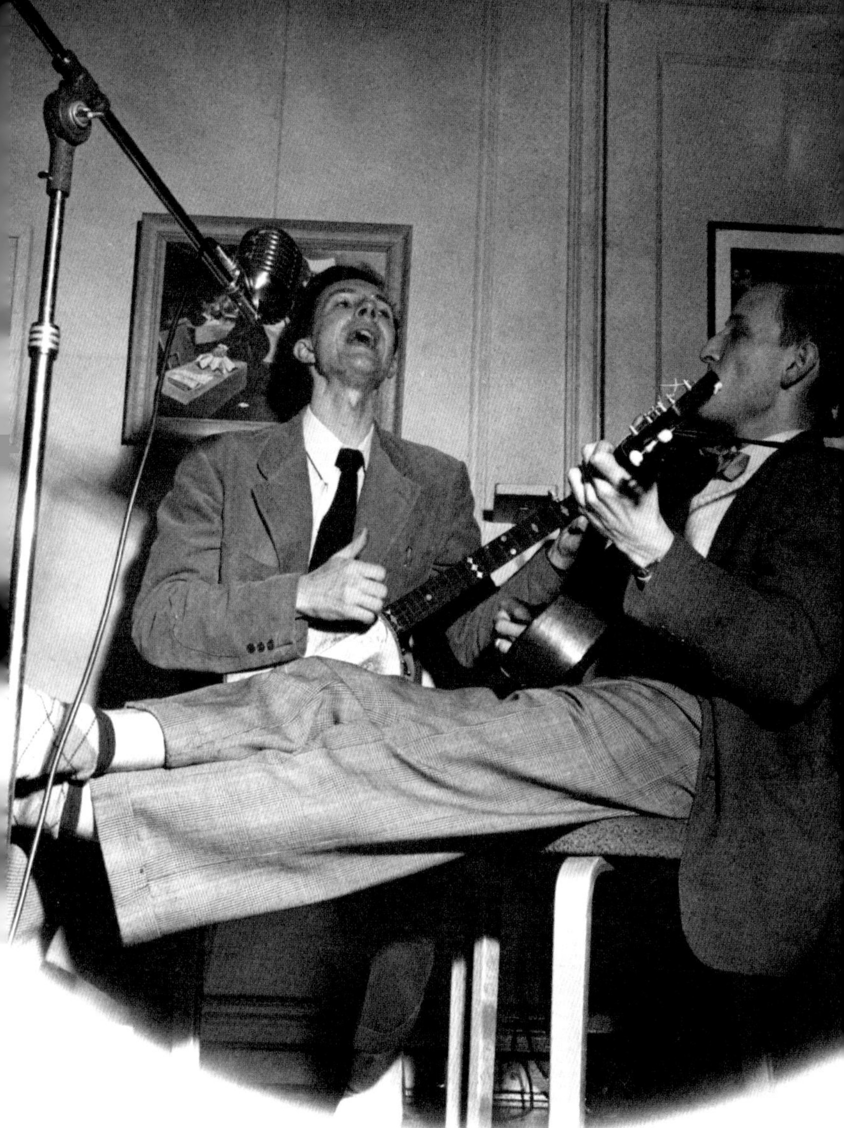

U

Unidentified Speaker Discussing the Historical, Cultural, and Educational Value of the Tony Schwartz Collection
Unidentified tape 37
United Airlines: Flight Comments

V

Valet
VD Jingle: "VD Is for Everyone"
Virgil Fox—Organ Week
Voice Lesson for Kayla
The Voices of Eight Presidents
Voodoo

W

Wake Up Story (Condensed Time Story)
Wanda Landowska
Weavers : 12-26-52: Reel #3
What Goes Zub Zub?
Where Have All the UFOs Gone?
Why Gwen Watson Came to New York City
Woman Screams
Women Cops Phone Call
Work Songs, Lampert Farm
Worry #1

Pete Seeger and Fred Hellerman of the Weavers, ca. 1952

RP-84-R WNYC YO-YO's IN N.Y.

3:53 6/8/71

ON a Saturday walk, Tony comes across some youngsters from Queens, who playing with their yo-yo's on Fifth Ave. They came to look at stamp and book shops. They can do; "Walk the dog","bite the dog ","around the world",and "Rock the baby." It is a lot of pocketsize fun.

Kids from uptown do;"Rifle man" and"eating spaghetti."

X

Xmas on Fifth Ave. & Peru

Y

Yip Harburg at Rosewalls, 1954-10-23
Yoram Kaniuk and Marlon Brando, 1952-11-19
Yo-Yos in N.Y.

Z

Zelda Funeral, 1993-01-26

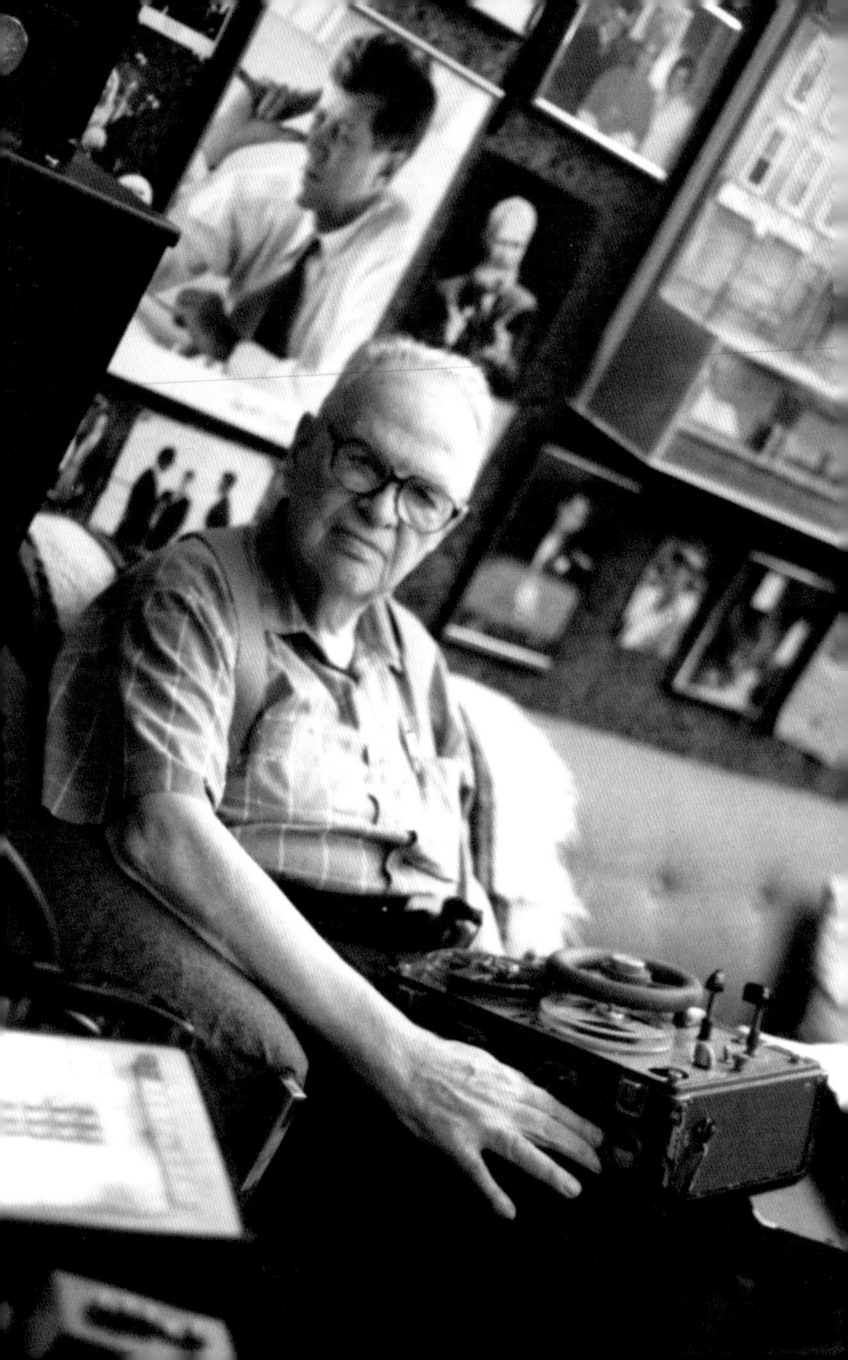

FURTHER LISTENING

This discography includes the main body of Tony Schwartz's known vinyl releases. All the albums originally issued on Folkways in the 1950s and 1960s remain available in digital format from Smithsonian Folkways Recordings. Many of the recordings listed here are available for listening on a variety of popular streaming platforms.

Titles preceded by an asterisk appear in this book.

**If He Asks You Was I Laughing*, 10" LP, Legend Recordings, 1952

**11 People*, 7", self-released, 1952

**1, 2, 3 and A Zing Zing Zing*, 10" LP, Folkways Records, 1953

**Moondog: On the Streets of New York*, 7", Mars, 1953

**Millions of Musicians*, 12" LP, Folkways Records, 1954

**New York 19*, 12" LP, Folkways Records, 1954

French Folk Songs, 10" LP, Folkways Records, 1954

**Nueva York*, 12" LP, Folkways Records, 1955

Exchange: Friendship Around the World Through Tape Exchange, 12" LP, Folkways Records, 1955

The Sound of Christmas, 12" LP, Storyboard, Inc., 1955

**Sounds of My City*, 10" LP, Folkways Records, 1956

**Music in the Streets*, 12" LP, Folkways Records, 1957

Tony Schwartz with portable tape recorder, ca. 2000

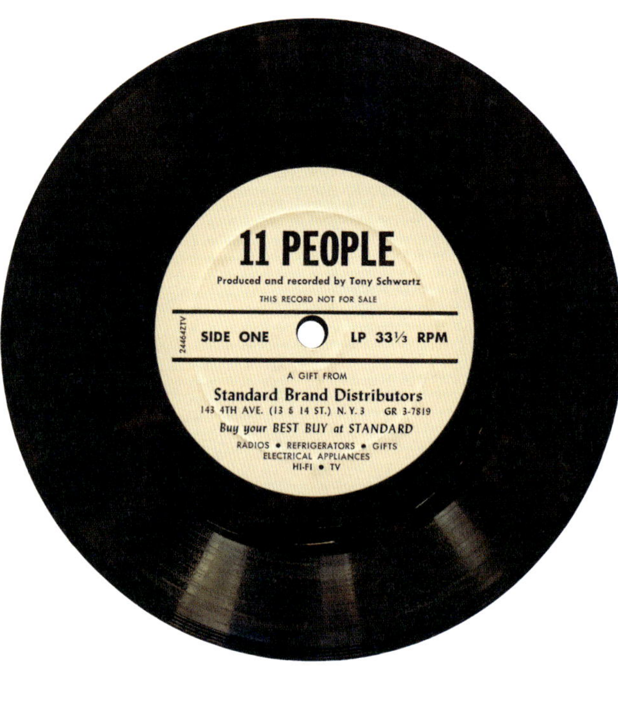
11 PEOPLE
Produced and recorded by Tony Schwartz
THIS RECORD NOT FOR SALE
24464ZTV
SIDE ONE
LP 33⅓ RPM
A GIFT FROM
Standard Brand Distributors
143 4TH AVE. (13 & 14 ST.) N. Y. 3 GR 3-7819
Buy your BEST BUY at STANDARD
RADIOS • REFRIGERATORS • GIFTS
ELECTRICAL APPLIANCES
HI-FI • TV

**An Actual Story in Sound of a Dog's Life*, 12" LP, Folkways Records, 1958

**Sound Effects, Volume One, City Sounds*, 12" LP, Folkways Records, 1958

**The World in My Mail Box*, 12" LP, Folkways Records, 1958

**The New York Taxi Driver*, 12" LP, Columbia Masterworks, 1959

That's My Opinion and It's Very True, 12" LP, self-released, 1959

The Story of New York, 10" LP, Legend Recordings, no date [1950s]

Season's Greetings from Consolidated Water Conditioning, 7", Consolidated Water Conditioning, no date [1950s]

**You're Stepping on My Shadow*, 12" LP, Folkways Records, 1962

The Sounds of the Family of Man, 12" LP, self-released, 1965

Standing Here at the Present Time . . . , 12" LP, self-released, 1965

Children and God a.k.a The Educated Eye II, 12" LP, self-released, 1966

A Popular Photography Presentation: Tony Schwartz on How to Record the Sound of Children, 12" LP, Capitol Custom, 1967

Martin Luther King at Local 1199, 12" LP, self-released, 1968

The Sound of Type / The Sound of Lettering, 7", self-released, year unknown [possibly 1969]

Digitized recordings of Schwartz's radio shows and other audio material are available for listening at the websites of WNYC and the Library of Congress.

SERIES EDITORS: CHRISTINE BURGIN AND ANDREW LAMPERT

Published by Christine Burgin Books
Ghent, New York

Special thanks to Matthew Barton, Curator, Recorded Sound, Library of Congress, Packard Campus for Audio Visual Conservation; Culpeper, VA; Recorded Sound Research Center, Library of Congress, Washington, D.C: Harrison Behl, Brian Cornell, and Laura Jeneman; Adam Stoltman, Ken Heyman Archive; New York Public Radio: Marcos Sueiro Bal; and with very special thanks to Anton Schwartz, Dawn Hagen, and Michaela Schwartz.

Front cover: Stan Cohen; page 4: Joseph Foldes; pages 10, 13, 28, 36, 51, 54, 60–61, 73, and 77: Andrew Lampert; pages 16, 24, and back cover: Ken Heyman

ISBN: 978-0-9976456-8-2

Published in 2026

www.furtherreadinglibrary.com

Copyedited, designed, and typeset in Caslon by Laura Lindgren
Proofread by Don Kennison
Image preparation by Lola Wegman
Front cover lettering by Craig Pettman
Printed on 115 gsm Kasadaka White
Printed in China

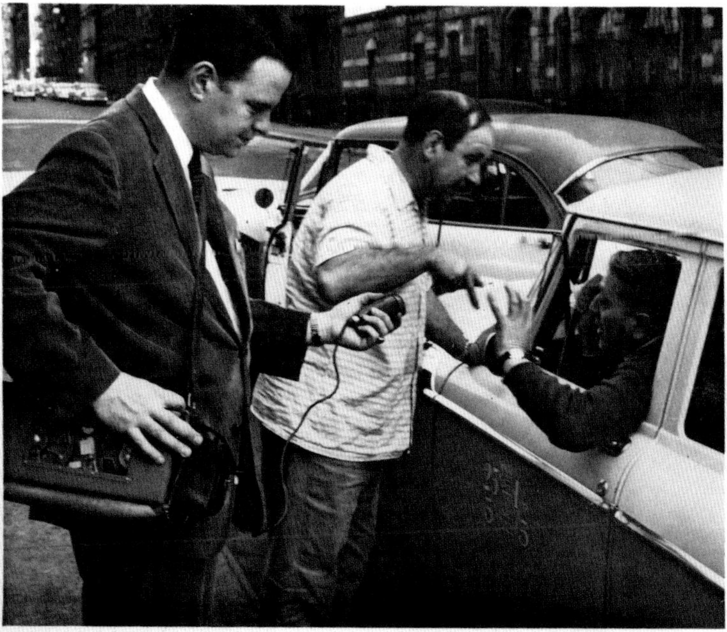

Why documentary recordist Tony Schwartz prefers tough, long-lasting tapes of Du Pont MYLAR®

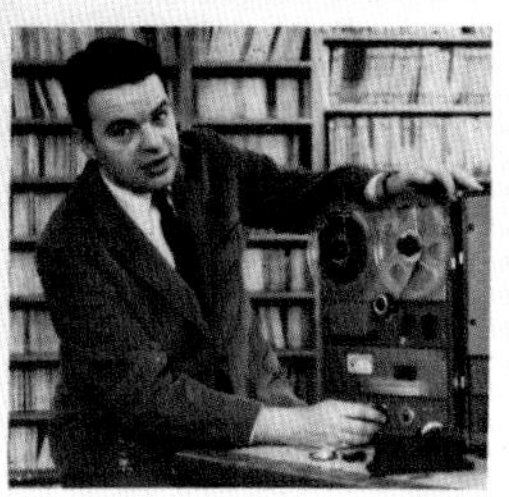

"The extra playing time offered by tapes of 'Mylar' lets me record more on a reel. This adds up to a big space saving in my growing tape library."

"Many of the sounds I record can never be duplicated," says Tony Schwartz. "To capture and keep them through the years, I must have tape that is extra-strong and unfailingly reliable. That's why I now record exclusively on tapes of 'Mylar'* polyester film.

"Tapes of 'Mylar' are the only ones that give me the protection I need—with a 300% safety margin against stretching. I've never had one break on me. What's more, these tough tapes don't need any special storage care."

Tony Schwartz, unique documentary recordist, has created numerous prize-winning records from thousands of tape-recorded sounds of everyday life and folk songs.

Before you buy your next reel of tape, compare the exclusive advantages of tapes of "Mylar". Then, like Tony Schwartz, ask your dealer for a reel of your favorite brand of tape made of "Mylar" polyester film.

*"Mylar" is Du Pont's registered trademark for its brand of polyester film. Du Pont manufactures "Mylar", not finished magnetic recording tape. Tapes of "Mylar" are made by all manufacturers.

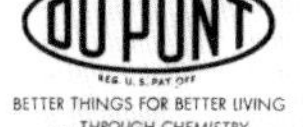

BETTER THINGS FOR BETTER LIVING
. . . THROUGH CHEMISTRY

DU PONT
MYLAR®
POLYESTER FILM

BE SURE OF SUPERIOR PERFORMANCE . . . LOOK FOR THE NAME "MYLAR" ON THE BOX

H. F. Tape Recording—1959
P. O. 9-784 ★ O 4-24-59

A-10669

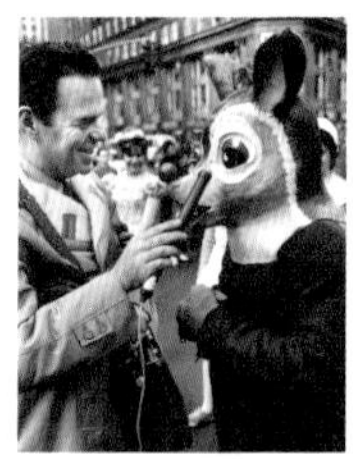

FRONT COVER: Tony Schwartz interviewing Rudolph at the Macy's Thanksgiving Day Parade, ca. 1960

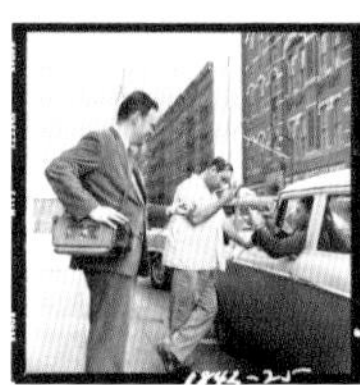

BACK COVER: Tony Schwartz interviewing a New York City taxi driver, 1959